HOW TO BUILD & DETAIL
Model Railroad
SCENES

LOU SASSI

KALMBACH
BOOKS

Printed in the United States of America

04 05 06 07 08 09 10 11 12 13   10 9 8 7 6 5 4 3 2 1

Visit our website at
http://kalmbachbooks.com
Secure online ordering available

Publishers Cataloging-In-Publication Data
(Prepared by The Donohue Group, Inc.)

Sassi, Lou.
    How to build and detail model railroad scenes / Lou Sassi.

    p.: ill. ; cm.
    Portion of title: Build and detail model railroad scenes
    ISBN: 0-89024-577-0

1. Railroads—Models. I. Title. II. Title: Build and detail model railroad scenes.

TF197 .S267 2004
625.1/9

Art Director: Kristi Ludwig
Book design: Sabine Beaupré

ACKNOWLEDGMENTS

I want to thank these people and manufacturers for helping make this book possible:

Marge Bailey (Wm. K. Walthers), Jim Elster (Scenic Express), Larry Galler (CS Designs), Bill Giacci (Classic Metal Works), Lee Karakas (Woodland Scenics), Loren Perry (Gold Medal Models), Bob and Ron Rands (Micro Engineering), Rick Rideout (Rix Power Products), Dale Rush (Blair Line), Jim Sacco (City Classics), Bruce Sparrow (Precision Laser Craft), Carol and Craig Vreeland (Sterling Models), and Martha Young (S.S. Limited).

Thanks also go to the folks at Activa Products, Evergreen Hills Models, GHQ, Grandt Line Products, NuComp Miniatures, Janes Trains, and Selley Finishing Touches.

Special thanks to Rich Cobb (the finest model builder in the good old U.S. of A.), Pete Darling, Dick Elwell, George Micklus, John Nehrich, Glen Sauter, and Jack Wright. And can't leave out Roger Carp and Kent Johnson at Kalmbach Publishing Co.

As always, an extra special thank you, with love, to my best friend and confidant—my wife, Cheryl.

CONTENTS

INTRODUCTION

In my first two Kalmbach books, *A Realistic HO Layout for Beginners* and *Basic Scenery for Model Railroaders*, I covered different aspects of scenery construction. For this, my third endeavor, the folks in Waukesha gave me free reign to delve into something I really enjoy—superdetailing model railroad scenery.

I've always felt that for a modeler to realistically create a miniature rendition of a scene or structure, he or she must have some concept of how and why that scene or structure was created in the real world. To model an industry, for example, you have to do a bit of research into how that industry functioned before you try to replicate it and its surroundings in miniature.

In this book I have tried to do some of that research for you. Where I found my own knowledge of a subject lacking, I turned to folks familiar with it for help.

For anyone who wants more information, I've included references to additional reading material. I have also tried to make it as easy as possible for you to get the materials I use by including the individual product number and the Walthers number where applicable.

This book has been an extremely enjoyable project for me. I hope you find the information I've provided both interesting and useful as you attempt to create a realistic miniature world around your own model railroad empire. Enjoy!

Lou Sassi

Meet me on

Detailing model railroad structures and scenes doesn't have to be reserved for expensive craftsman kits. In this chapter I'll discuss how I created and detailed a city block of inexpensive plastic structures on my HO scale home layout, the Boston & Maine West Hoosic Division Railroad.

The block in question is located in the city of Adams on my layout. I built Adams on a peninsula so that visitors can easily see all sides of the buildings. To some modelers, having to detail entire structures rather than just one or two sides may seem like a liability rather than an asset. However, seeing the structures from every angle helps draw viewers into the scene.

the corner

Fig. 1-1: In this aerial view of Main Street in Adams, we can see the alleyway between the park on the left and the Del Negro Pharmacy on the right.

Fig. 1-2: Moving around the scene, we're now in the back of the pharmacy. In the foreground is the rail siding to B. Saulet Company and Micklus Paint Company. The porches, steps, and litter add visual interest to the scene.

To show you the advantages of seeing structures from several perspectives, let's look at another part of Adams. Figure 1-1 shows Main Street. As viewers study the fronts of the structures, they notice an alleyway along the side of the building on the right. They see that alley pass beside and then behind the buildings, where they also find an array of doors, stairways, porches, and other details that add visual interest (fig. 1-2).

WALK AROUND THE BLOCK

Changes in elevation as well as obtuse and acute (rather than 90-degree) angles on a horizontal plane also add interest to a scene. I've found this is especially true with street scenes.

Let's consider the block that I'll describe in this chapter (shown in fig. 1-3). (Bear in mind that there are no changes in elevation along the railroad siding, Bieniek Avenue, and the first 65 feet of Main Street.)

Starting in the upper left-hand corner, we go east (to the right) along the railroad tracks about 49 feet. The property line then makes a 10-degree angle to the left, and we continue east another 65 feet. The corner where the tracks meet Bieniek Avenue is a 70-degree turn to the right.

The property line follows Bieniek Avenue south for 30 feet. It then makes a 110-degree turn to the

right and follows Main Street west for 65 feet. Here the line makes an angular change of 5 degrees to the left and starts to drop vertically.

When we reach the corner of Main Street and Railroad Avenue, we've gone about 58 feet west and dropped about 11 feet. From this corner we turn 60 degrees to the north (right) and follow Railroad Avenue about 48 feet back to our point of origin. Figure 1-4 shows the scene with the tracks, sidewalks, and roads in place.

I decided to use five inexpensive plastic kits for the HO scale buildings within this block (see fig. 1-5).

They are the Atlas no. 150-704 Signal Tower; Design Preservation Models nos. 243-101 Kelly's Saloon, 243-105 Skip's Chicken and Ribs, and 243-108 Goodfellows Hall; and Smalltown USA no. 699-6013 Vivian's Family Shoe Store.

All of these structures, when built unaltered, are perfectly rectangular boxes (fig. 1-6). Therefore, we'll make some alterations so they fit our oddly shaped block. The changes I have in mind are relatively easy to do. Besides, even if you mess up, you're dealing with kits that each cost less than $10, so your pocketbook isn't hit too hard.

Fig. 1-3: Here we see the various angles and distances that make up our city block. Note in the upper sketch that there's also a vertical drop to the corner of Main Street and Railroad Avenue. These odd angles and elevation changes add visual interest.

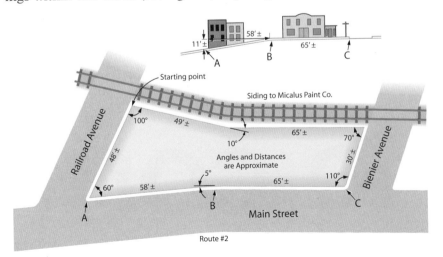

Fig. 1-4: Here we see the city block awaiting the installation of the structures.

Fig. 1-5: The five structures we will use for the scene are (from left to right) Design Preservation Models no. 243-105 Skip's Chicken and Ribs, Smalltown USA no. 699-6013 Vivian's Family Shoe Store, DPM no. 243-101 Kelly's Saloon, DPM no. 243-108 Goodfellows Hall, and Atlas no. 150-704 Signal Tower.

Fig. 1-6: Placing these out-of-the-box structures into position indicates that we need to do some alterations to make them properly fit in their locations.

SKIP-A-DEE-DO-DAH

Skip's Chicken and Ribs is a good example of how I alter a structure to fit a location. A note of caution: one problem you must contend with when altering a building is the location of existing doors and windows. Study all the walls of a kit before making any cuts so you don't end up cutting an opposite wall in the middle of a window or door.

Once I decided where I wanted to make my cuts, I removed a section of the wall by scribing it repeatedly with a hobby knife using an inverted X-acto no. 11 blade (fig. 1-7). After scribing about halfway through the material, I gripped the piece firmly with both hands and snapped it apart (fig. 1-8).

I removed cast-on details, like a cornice bracket, by slicing them off with an X-acto no. 17 blade (fig. 1-9). Figure 1-10 shows the building and removed wall sections.

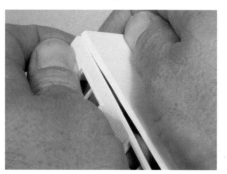

Fig. 1-7: Here I'm scribing a sidewall of Skip's Chicken and Ribs with the backside of an X-acto no. 11 blade.

Fig. 1-8: After scribing halfway through the material, I snap the piece apart.

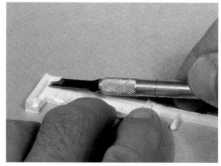

Fig. 1-9: A cast-on cornice bracket is sliced off the casting using an X-acto no. 17 blade.

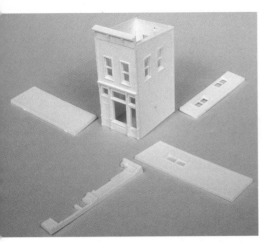

Fig. 1-10: Here's the new Skip's Chicken and Ribs, along with its discarded wall sections.

Fig. 1-11: The front three-quarter view of Skip's shows the styrene extensions to the front columns. Vollmer brick foundation, cut to conform to the elevation change, makes a great source of window details and roof details.

Fig. 1-12: The rear three-quarter view of Skip's shows the styrene strip stock wall caps, styrene scuppers, brass tubing downspouts and vent pipes, sandpaper roof, and scrap-box chimney.

Figs.1-13, 1-14, 1-15, and 1-16: In these photos we see the altered structure on the left and the stock kit on the right.

Once I had glued together the building's abbreviated walls, I added Holgate & Reynolds and Vollmer brick foundation, strip styrene trim, K&S Engineering brass tubing for downspouts and vent pipes, a sandpaper roof, and a chimney left from another kit (see figs. 1-11 and 1-12).

Figures 1-13, 1-14, 1-15, and 1-16 show the altered structure on the left and the stock kit on the right. I took the window dressings for Skip's and the other buildings from the Signs, Posters & Storefront sets available from Rensselaer Railroad Shops.

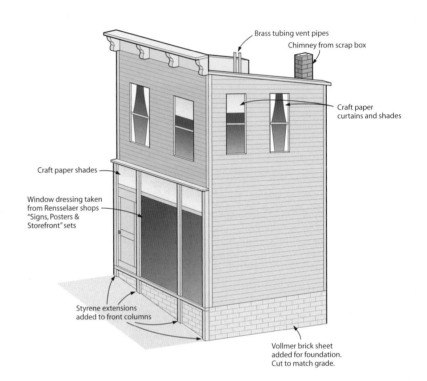

Brass tubing vent pipes

Chimney from scrap box

Craft paper curtains and shades

Craft paper shades

Window dressing taken from Rensselaer shops "Signs, Posters & Storefront" sets

Styrene extensions added to front columns

Vollmer brick sheet added for foundation. Cut to match grade.

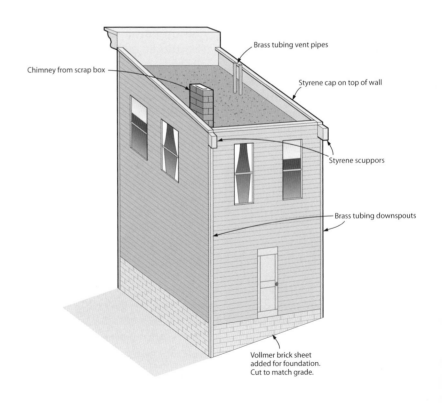

Chimney from scrap box

Brass tubing vent pipes

Styrene cap on top of wall

Styrene scuppors

Brass tubing downspouts

Vollmer brick sheet added for foundation. Cut to match grade.

ONWARD WE GO

I used the same approach for altering the rest of the structures. In fig. 1-17 we see Vivian's Family Shoe Store with a piece of Vollmer stone wall used for a foundation. On top of the stone is a piece of cardboard cut at an angle. I used this piece as a template to cut the stonework to fit the drop in the street along the side of the building.

Figure 1-18 shows the stock structure on the right and the altered and detailed building on the left. In fig. 1-19 you see how I used a vintage ad (more in fig. 1-20) to create a billboard on one wall of the building. I buy old magazines at flea markets, antique shops, and yard sales for about 25 cents each.

I altered Kelly's Saloon and Goodfellows Hall in a manner similar to what I did to Skip's. They are shown in stock and kitbashed form in figs. 1-21 and 1-22.

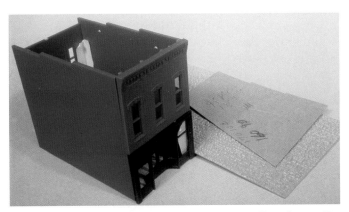

Fig. 1-17: Here's the Smalltown USA Vivian's Family Shoe Store with a section of Vollmer stone wall that will be used to create a foundation for it on the right.

Fig. 1-18: The stock structure is on the right, and the altered building is on the left.

Fig. 1-19: Gluing an ad from a period magazine to the wall of the building creates a large billboard.

Fig. 1-20: Old magazines are a great source of material for period advertisements. These came from a yard sale and cost about a quarter each.

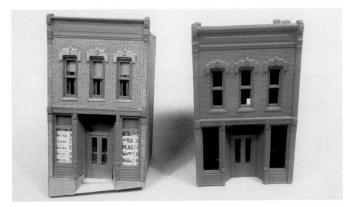

Fig. 1-21: Kelly's Saloon in basic kit form on the right and altered to fit the scene on the left.

Fig. 1-22: Goodfellows Hall in stock form on the right and modified to fit the city block on the left.

TOWER OF POWER

Jimmy's Diner is a different story. It reflects the influence of John Nehrich on my modeling and his work on the NEB&W HO scale layout at Rensselaer Polytechnic Institute in Troy, New York. I've always been amazed at his ingenuity when it comes to kitbashing components of a building into something completely unrelated to the original structure.

I followed John's approach when designing Jimmy's Diner. I needed a small, one-story building to fill the gap created by the odd angle at the corner of Main Street and Bieniek Avenue (on the right in fig. 1-3).

I took an Atlas signal tower that had been gathering dust in my basement for about a decade. After studying the structure, I realized that the wooden second floor would make a nice clapboard-sided one-story diner.

Figure 1-23 below illustrates the results of my work. The second-floor door of the tower is now the front door of the diner. The wall to the left on the tower, along with the remainder of the wall to which the doorway was attached, is now the long (right) sidewall of the diner. I used a third wall to create the back wall of the diner (fig. 1-24).

I built a cardboard roof and added some vents and a sign. Then I threw the remaining tower wall into my scrap box for future use.

Fig. 1-23: The top floor of the Atlas Signal Tower on the right became Jimmy's Diner on the left.

Fig. 1-24: This side-view of Jimmy's Diner shows the various wall sections used to make up the structure.

THEORIZING FOR THE FAINT OF HEART

With all the structures out of the way, let's get back to some scenery "theory." I never intended to fill the entire block with buildings. Instead, the area between Kelly's Saloon and Goodfellows Hall was going to be a vacant lot created by the demolition of a building due to fire or abandonment. Remember, there's a siding running along the rear of the property.

This lot enables viewers to see a train pass between the existing buildings on its way to and from the industries along the spur. With an opportunity to fill the lot with the trash that accumulates in such an area, I can create an interesting scene in less time than it would take to assemble another structure.

Figure 1-25 shows drums and barrels, along with discarded corrugated metal panels lying about the lot. A pile of rusted metal lies next to the corrugated panels. I mined this from the bottom of a water heater that a friend had discarded. (Proof that hobby shops aren't the only sources for miniature details.)

The sidewall of Goodfellows has the first-floor window bricked up because there was once another structure butted against it. The brick is still red because it wouldn't have been possible to paint it tan like the remainder of Goodfellows when the demolished building was still standing.

Notice the remnants of tarpaper roof on the side of Goodfellows.

This is what remains of the roof of the demolished building. I did this by dabbing Duco Cement along the sidewall and painting it flat black.

To the rear of the lot is an old wooden fence. There is a panel removed and a well-worn path from the sidewalk to the opening. This represents a shortcut created by some neighborhood kids.

There are still remnants of the brick walls of the demolished building running at ground level along the side of Goodfellows and just in front of the fence at the rear. I created this effect by cutting out sections of Vollmer brick sheet and gluing them in place. Figure 1-26 shows the back of the lot with the accumulation of more junk along the fence and the path continuing along the side of Skip's.

TOOLBOX

Downspouts
K&S Engineering no. 370-1008
1/16" brass tubing

Foundations
Evergreen no. 269-9105 .040" sheet
    styrene
Vollmer no. 770-6028 brick sheet
Vollmer no. 770-6031 stone sheet

Lot Details and Fence
Alloy Forms no. 119-2002
    barrels
Campbell no. 200-804
    corrugated aluminum sheets
Northeast Scale Lumber no. 521-
    3014 2 x 8
Northeast Scale Lumber no. 521-
    3030 4 x 4

Fig. 1-25: Rather than add another building between Kelly's and Goodfellows, I opted for a lot that was left vacant after another structure supposedly burned and was then torn down. This let me add details (trash) to the lot while giving viewers an opportunity to see the rail action beyond the remaining structures.

Fig. 1-26: The same scene from the opposite side of the tracks. Note the missing board in the fence, most likely removed by local kids so they could take a shortcut to the rail yard.

Down on the

F arms have been an integral part of the American landscape for centuries, and they look great on an HO scale layout. A convincing farm scene depends on having the right buildings and ancillary items.

To decide how to create such a scene, you must know the purpose of your miniature farm. Research is necessary to understand how farms looked and operated in the region and period of your railroad.

By the middle of the 19th century, farms had, thanks to the agricultural revolution, moved beyond subsistence. Productivity increased to the point that farmers could specialize and then distribute their commodities to local and distant markets. Railroads played a crucial role in this transformation.

Rutland RS-1 no. 403 rolls past Peavey Farm on the main line between Rutland and Burlington, Vermont. I based that farm on Brookmont Farm, once owned by the family of my friend Rich Cobb.

farm

My layout is set in New England, a region that was heavily farmed in the 18th and 19th centuries. When farmers in this area realized that new agricultural machinery did not work well in the rocky soil, they began to specialize in dairy farming. (Wisconsin later turned to dairy farming for the same reason).

Because I was born and reared in the city, I turned to my friend, former farm kid Rich Cobb, to help explain the layout of a typical dairy farm and the function of the different buildings usually found there.

Figure 2-1 illustrates the actual farm complex (Brookmont Farm) Rich recalls while fig. 2-2 shows how I selectively compressed it for my diorama.

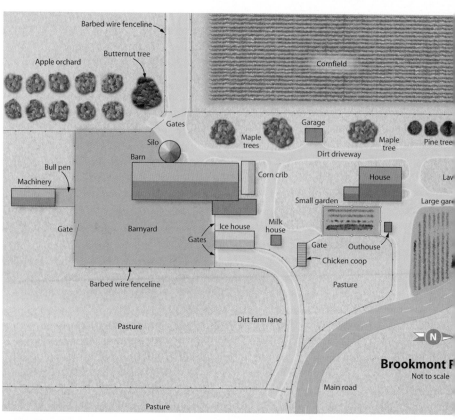

Fig. 2-1: The layout of the real Brookmont Farm complex.

Fig. 2-2: The condensed version of the Brookmont Farm complex.

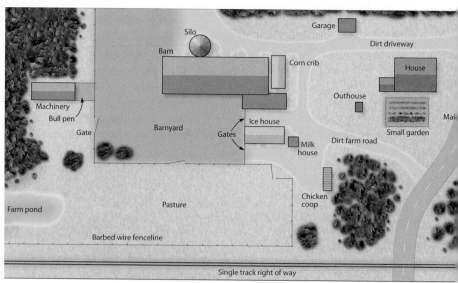

BROOKMONT FARM (AS REMEMBERED BY RICH COBB)

Ours was typical of dairy farms in the Northeast during the last half of the 19th and first half of the 20th century. Most were small family farms, with only enough acres and cows so that one man could handle the work. Later, as sons became available to help with the chores, more land was acquired and barns expanded to hold more cattle.

Brookmont Farm was located in Warwick, New York. The barn was built in 1847 (the date is carved in the hay mow floor), and, presumably, the original house was built about the same time.

The farm consisted of about 68 acres, most of which was used to grow corn or hay or was used as pastures. There was also an apple orchard (not modeled) behind the barn. Most of the lower fields were drained by open ditches that ran into a brook which fed the pond; however there were two swampy areas that were not tilled.

My grandfather bought the farm in 1910. The original house burned in 1913. The new house (the one that's modeled) was evidently built on the same stone foundation as the original, although half of the cellar was cement block with a cement

Brookmont Farm as seen in the late 1940s.

Bird's-eye view of the barn. Farmer Cobb heads for the fields on his (GHQ) tractor pulling a (GHQ) manure spreader. The hay loader has been stored next to the ice-house for the time being.

The wood-sided barn measured 72 feet long and 30 feet wide and had a 10 x 20 foot L-shaped extension at the north end. Note the 15-foot-square concrete milk house.

floor and the other half was a dirt floor. My uncle started renting the farm from my grandfather in 1941 and purchased it 11 years later.

The barn was modified over the years as needed. For example, the extension on the northeast corner originally contained box stalls for workhorses. My uncle purchased a John Deere Model B tractor in 1941 and shortly after the need for horses was a thing of the past. He bought a Farmall F-12 tractor in the late 1940s and then a John Deere Model 50 in 1956.

The extension on the south end of the barn, added in 1946, made it easier to clean the barn and gave additional space for storing hay. Two years later, the wall of the horse barn was replaced with cement blocks. Box stalls for calves were also built inside. The cement block milk house was also added in 1948, ending the chore of carrying milk to a separate wood structure. Finally, a cement silo was added in 1951 to store corn silage.

The Barn

The barn had two rows of stalls for cows that faced each other with an alley between them for feeding. There were 33 cow stalls in all. The inside of the barn was whitewashed every few years, and an insecticide was often mixed with the whitewash to reduce the number of flies.

Milking was done with vacuum-powered milking machines and occasionally by hand when the power went off. The cows were fed feed purchased in 100-pound bags, hay from the haymow, and corn silage after the silo was built.

Manure from the cows was originally shoveled by hand into a wheelbarrow and then dumped into a spreader for spreading onto the fields. But in the late 1940s an overhead track was installed. This track carried a bucket that ran on a trolley. The bucket was lowered using a chain fall arrangement and manure was shoveled into it. It was then raised and pushed out over the spreader to be dumped.

The upper level of the barn, the haymow, was where hay was stored during the summer to be fed to the cows in the winter. In the early days, hay was loaded onto wagons by hand or with a hay loader, which was pulled behind the wagon.

The loaded wagon was pulled into the barn where a hay fork, which ran on the track in the peak of the roof, was lowered to pick up the hay, similar to a clamshell bucket on a steam shovel.

A rope and a series of pulleys, pulled either by horses or a tractor, moved the fork up to the peak of the roof and then horizontally to the right or left, depending on how the pulleys were set, until it was over the correct mow, where the fork was tripped. For feeding, the hay was forked by hand down through the hatches in the barn floor and distributed to the cows.

Some farms hired people with large hay balers to bale the hay. The hay was brought to the baler close to the barn, where it was then run through the machine and formed into compact bales. The bales were then stored in the haymow.

The advantage of this method was that the hay took up less space and was much easier to handle. In the 1940s, smaller hay balers were developed that could be pulled behind a tractor in the field. This soon became the accepted practice for putting up hay.

Two types of hay balers were available. The more common one produced rectangular bales. Allis-Chalmers developed a machine

The original 8 x 9 foot milk house was a separate structure with clapboard siding.

The icehouse was 15 x 30 feet and had clapboard siding and a gable roof.

The 11 x 22 foot corncrib had wood sides that tapered to 8 feet at the base.

that, through a series of rollers and wide belts, rolled the hay into round bales.

The benefit of this new machine was that if the hay got wet before it was taken to the barn, only the outer layer of the bale was spoiled. A disadvantage was that the tractor had to stop when each bale was finished to discharge it from the baler. Also, the round bales tended to roll off the wagons, making it a necessity to put up sides on the wagons.

Rectangular bales won out in the 1950s. By the mid-1960s, kickers on the balers had been developed that threw the bales into a wagon towed behind the baler.

The Milk House
Milk was carried in open pails to the milk house. Here it was poured through a metal strainer with a cloth filter into metal cans. Full cans were placed in a cooler until they were taken to a creamery—a daily chore. Prior to purchasing a milk cooler that had an electrical cooling unit, ice from the icehouse was used to cool the milk.

Originally, the milk house was located a good distance from the barn for sanitary reasons. However, the development of sanitizers and insecticides eliminated this need, and by the mid-1950s, most barns had a milk house attached.

Bulk milk handling had become widespread by this time as well. Milk could now be poured into a

large stainless-steel tank in the milk house, which had a built-in cooling system.

Tank trucks came to the farm, pumped out the milk, and took it to the creamery. They usually arrived every other day, depending on the cows' production and the capacity of the tank.

The Icehouse
Prior to electrification and the development of coolers, ice was cut from the farm pond in winter and hauled to an insulated building called the icehouse. This provided ice for cooling the milk. It also provided ice for the family's icebox (before refrigerators became in common use).

By the 1940s, the icehouse was no longer used for ice storage. As a result, the ground level was converted into calf pens and the upper level was used to store hay.

The Corncrib
Corn was grown on most farms to use for feed, and the ears were stored in the corncrib until they were ground into feed. The corncrib was elevated on large stones or cement piers to keep out rodents, and the walls were built of slats with spaces between them to allow air to circulate for drying. The slats were lined on the inside with chicken wire to keep the corncobs from falling out and to keep the rodents from coming in.

The Bull Pen / Machinery Shed
Most bulls were kept away from the cows, whether in a small box stall in the barn or a separate shed. This may or may not have added to the bulls' mean temperament. Cows were brought to the breeding rack as necessary. The rest of the shed had large sliding doors and a dirt floor, where machinery was kept when it wasn't being used.

The Silo
Many farms had wood silos constructed of vertical boards held together with rods, which were tightened with turnbuckle-like devices to hold everything together. These rods were spaced closely together at the bottom, where the most pressure from the contents was exerted. As the rings of rods moved up, they were spaced farther apart as there was less pressure.

The same principle applied to water tanks. The late 1940s saw the development of cement silos, which were more durable than wood. These were constructed of 1 x 3 foot cast concrete slabs with tongue-and-groove edges.

A cement foundation was poured, and the first row of slabs stood on edge around a circular metal frame with the tongue-and-groove edges interlocked. Rods and turnbuckles held the slabs together. The metal form was raised, and the next row installed.

This process was repeated until the desired height was reached. Typical silos were 12 to 20 feet in diameter, and many reached 60 feet in height. The rounded top was formed of sheet metal or aluminum. The insides of the silo were coated with a material to seal the cracks and prevent the acid in the silage from attacking the concrete.

Corn was either cut by hand in the field or with a tractor-drawn cutter that cut the cornstalks off at the ground level and tied them together in bundles. The bundles were loaded by hand onto a wagon and brought to the silo.

A belt driven chopper/blower was located at the silo. It had a chain conveyor that pulled the bundles into the chopper, which was essentially a 4-foot-diameter fan with sharp knives on the blades. This cut the corn into small pieces, and the fan blew the corn up a pipe into the top of the silo.

Tractor-drawn choppers were later developed. They chopped the corn in the field and blew it into wagons. The wagons had four enclosed sides, sometimes a roof, and a belt or chain mechanism on the floor to unload the corn. These were pulled to the silo where the corn was unloaded into a blower, which blew it up into the silo.

The covered ladder going up the side of the silo adjacent to the barn had a series of doors. A farmer climbed up to the door that corresponded to the level of the silage and threw down the necessary amount for a feeding with a silage fork.

The 1960s saw the development of silage unloaders. One style rested on top of the silage. It had an auger that pivoted in the center of the silo and moved around like the hands of a clock pulling the silage to the center, where a small blower threw the silage though a door, where it fell to ground level.

A second style of unloader was developed with the steel (fiber-glass lined) silos of the 1960s. It had a permanent auger mounted in the bottom of the silo that also pivoted in the center and moved around

Some of the farm equipment sits in the shade around the machinery shed waiting for its next call to duty.

Made of concrete blocks, the 20 x 42 foot bull pen/machine storage barn was one-story high with a shed roof.

The 63-foot-high silo was fashioned out of interlocking concrete blocks. It measured 18 feet in diameter at the base and 16 feet at the top.

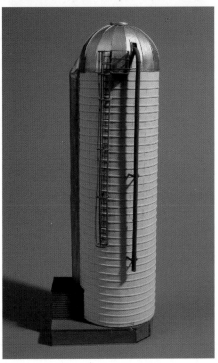

like clock hands. A second auger brought the material out of the silo and placed the silage on a feed cart to be taken to feed the cows.

The Farm House

This main structure was also modified over the years on Brookmont Farm. In the 1940s a back porch was added. It contained an entryway, a place for a washing machine (the kind with the wringers), and a second bathroom. Underneath was a storage area for wood for the fireplace and the stove in the kitchen.

The main floor consisted of the kitchen, living room, and two front rooms, which my grandfather used as an antique shop after he retired from farming. The inventory eventually outgrew the space, and a large front porch was enclosed with windows and shelves to hold additional antiques. Upstairs were four bedrooms, a bathroom, and a stairway going up to the attic.

The Chicken Coop

There were two small coops that each held about 20 chickens. This was enough to produce eggs for the family and an occasional Sunday dinner. My uncle lived in a small house (not modeled) at the foot of the hill. Behind this structure was a small brooder house that was

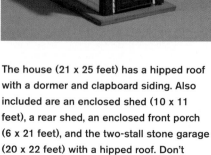

The house (21 x 25 feet) has a hipped roof with a dormer and clapboard siding. Also included are an enclosed shed (10 x 11 feet), a rear shed, an enclosed front porch (6 x 21 feet), and the two-stall stone garage (20 x 22 feet) with a hipped roof. Don't forget the outhouse (6 x 7 feet) with clapboard siding.

Here we can see the garden, outhouse, doghouse, and garage. The dog is a Preiser product, the picket fence is by Central Valley, and the vegetables are small bits of Woodland Scenics and Scenic Express ground foam. The washer and trash cans come from SS Limited and the rural mailbox is from Selley Finishing Touches.

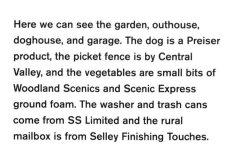

heated with electric lamps and insulated for raising baby chicks.

There was also a long chicken house for a couple hundred chickens and a two-story steel building that was originally a chicken house but later became a storage building for antique furniture.

During the 1940s and 1950s, my uncle had a thriving egg business that supplied fresh eggs to a local grocery store. This came to an end, however, with the development of large poultry farms.

The Livestock

Many farmers prefer to stay with one breed of cows, and many have registered herds. My uncle, for example, raised Holsteins. Other popular breeds are Jerseys, Ayrshires, and Guernseys, which are reddish brown and white.

There are several varieties of chickens. They vary in color from reddish-brown to brown, black, and white.

Many farms also have a pigpen where hogs are kept. Some have small herds of sheep or goats and flocks of ducks or geese.

Finally, back in the 1940s and 1950s, some farms still kept work-horses because they needed them. Riding horses were also common.

Farmer Cobb heads for the fields with a manure spreader in tow.

The 9 x 20 foot chicken coop was a simple wood-sided structure.

COW TRACKS IN "GROUND GOOP"

Anyone who has read my other books is aware of my obsession with a material called "Ground Goop." It's a mix of 1 cup Celluclay, 1 cup Vermiculite, ⅔ cup Elmer's white glue, and 1 cup Pittsburgh Tobacco Brown flat house paint. I dump in a jigger of concentrated Lysol to prevent mildew and add enough water to allow the mix to be spread with an artist's spatula.

One of the reasons I like Ground Goop so much is its workability. I can add ruts to roads, erosion to hillsides and, in this case, cow tracks into muddy ponds. I simply spread a ⅛" thick layer of Ground Goop around my pond and use a length of small-diameter solid wire to poke holes in it to resemble cow tracks (fig. 2-9).

I sprinkle on some fine dirt and fix the whole shebang with a spray of diluted matte medium. After waiting a couple days for it to dry, I add cows (fig. 2-10).

A light breeze causes ripples on the pond as three girls head down to the water for a drink on this warm summer afternoon. Rich's scratchbuilt New Idea Company gates look great.

Fig. 2-9: Use a length of wire to create cow prints in the Ground Goop.

Fig. 2-10: Place the cows in position.

READY TO MODEL

There you have it—an in-depth look at the Brookmont Farm complex and its different structures. For us modelers, the key word is *complex*. This farm, like thousands of others throughout the country, was producing agricultural goods not only for the market but also for the family themselves.

Even though this was a dairy farm, the family did raise chickens and had an apple orchard. There were also two gardens on the property. The larger one likely supplied a family-run vegetable stand, while the smaller one provided food for the family.

A hay loader, pulled by a tractor (figs. 2-3 and 2-4), was also used on this farm. Hay was raked into winrows and left to dry for two or three days. Then a tractor pulling a hay wagon with a hay loader hooked behind picked up the hay.

REFERENCES

Nehrich, John. *Guide to Farms and Farm Buildings.* www.railroad.union.rpi.edu/images/structures/Farms.asp

Noble, Allen George. *The Old Barn Book: A Field Guide to North American Barns and Other Farm Structures* (Rutgers University Press).

Fig. 2-3: Three-quarter view of a scratchbuilt hay loader (14 feet long and 8 feet wide).

Fig. 2-4: The other side of the hay loader.

Fig. 2-5: Rich Cobb's cousin works on a hay loader in the 1940s.

Rotating teeth on the bars on the back of the hay loader picked up the winrow, and moving bars on the eccentric slid the hay to the top of the loader, where it fell down a chute onto the wagon. Figure 2-5 shows Rich Cobb's cousin working with a hay loader in the 1940s.

Also important for any farm scene are gates. Those seen in the opening photo were made by New Idea Company, which also made farm machinery. Orange and green were that firm's colors of choice. Gates were also made and sold by Grange League Federation, which became a part of Agway in 1964.

So now we're ready to develop our own farm scene. There are many possible structures to consider on the market now. Here is a selection, with their numbers taken from the most recent Walthers HO scale catalog.

TOOLBOX

Barns
Alpine Division Scale Models no. 700-87 Mail Pouch Tobacco Barn
American Model Builders no. 152-119 Country Barn
Bachmann no. 160-45151 Barn
Bachmann no. 160-45152 Farm Buildings with Animals
JV Models no. 345-2001 Gable Roof Dairy Barn
Model Power no. 490-601

Farmhouses
American Model Builders no. 152-140 Two-Story Farmhouse
Atlas no. 150-711 Kate's Colonial Home
Walthers Cornerstone no. 933-3601 Aunt Lucy's House

Silos
Alder Models (Box 1537, Deep River, ON Canada K0J 1P0; 613-584-3149; www.magma.ca/~alder) Farm Silo Kits (concrete and wood)
International Hobby Corp. no. 348-225 Farm Silo
JV Models no. 345-2000 Farm Silo

Garages
Blair Line no. 184-173 One-Car Garage
Depots by John no. 87-122 Garage

Outhouses
Blair Line no. 87-132 Two-Hole Outhouse
Woodland Scenics no. 785-214 Outhouse with Man

Corncrib
SS Limited no. 650-1156 Country Corn Crib

Chicken Coop
Woodland Scenics no. 785-215 Chicken Coop

Icehouse
Woodland Scenics no. 785-219 Ice House

Tractors and Farm Machinery
Athearn no. 140-7700 John Deere Model B Tractor
Athearn no. 140-7701 John Deere Model 50 Tractor
GHQ no. 284-60001 International Super M Tractor
GHQ no. 284-60002 Manure Spreader
GHQ no. 284-60003 Three-Bottom Plow
GHQ no. 284-60005 Super M Tractor with Front Loader
GHQ no. 284-60008 Bin Wagon
Life-Like no. 433-1650 International Super M Tractor
Woodland Scenics no. 785-207 Disc Plow
Woodland Scenics no. 785-208 Seeder

Farm Animals
Preiser no. 590-14150 Black and White Cows
Preiser no. 590-14168 Chickens
Woodland Scenics no. 785-841 Dogs and Cats

WEATHERING VERTICAL WOOD SIDING

The barn on my HO farm, like other buildings, is made of vertical board siding. It's easy to make the basswood sheet siding resemble individual boards by using a combination of India ink stains and denatured alcohol wipes.

I start by airbrushing the building with Floquil no. 270-110450 SOO Red. Then I stain individual boards with a small soft bristle brush dipped into a mix of 1 pint rubbing alcohol and 1 teaspoon India ink (fig. 2-6). By varying the number of applications to individual boards, each takes on a slightly different tone.

Next, as seen in fig. 2-7, I randomly wipe boards with a soft cotton cloth dipped in paint thinner (denatured alcohol). This gradually removes some of the stain and paint. You can see the results in fig. 2-8.

Fig. 2-6: Apply India Ink to side of barn with small soft bristle brush.

Fig. 2-7: Rub off the ink and paint randomly from the boards.

Fig. 2-8: The barn siding stained and weathered to different degrees looks much more like individual boards than a sheet of scribed wood does.

A factory with

The first "factories" in the United States were devoted to grinding grain. Even though the Industrial Revolution introduced ever larger factories producing a myriad of finished goods, the word "mill" was, and still is, used to describe them.

The mill I'll discuss in this chapter, Peerless Tanning Company, served the leather industry a short distance from my family's home in Gloversville, New York. As the name implies, Gloversville was a hotbed of leather production, glove manufacturing in particular, in the 19th and early 20th centuries.

Rutland engine no. 403 heads down trackage on Fulton Street in Burlington, Vermont, passing Peerless Tanning Company, as a local youngster checks the power plant of his 1932 Ford coupe.

out peers

Fig. 3-1: A view of the prototype Peerless Tanning Company taken at the northeast corner.

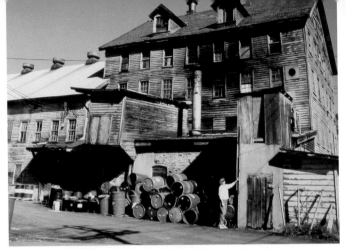

Fig. 3-2: Another view of the prototype building taken from the southeast. Note the multitude of barrels and pallets around the rear.

Fig. 3-3: A close-up of the many barrels piled along the rear of the building.

Today, unfortunately, due to increased competition from foreign manufacturers, Gloversville and its sister city of Johnstown (where Peerless is located) are mere shadows of their former selves. The prototype photos of the real Peerless were taken in 1999, not long before it was abandoned.

Figures 3-1 and 3-2 show the Peerless mill in its final years when it was suffering from the ravages of time and neglect. As a modeler, I like the challenge of replicating in miniature the look of this prototype's deteriorating condition.

Another thing to note in my photos (especially fig. 3-3) is the clutter that accumulates around an operating leather mill. A modeler should understand at least the basic workings of a particular industry before he or she can realistically replicate its environs.

UP ON THE ROOF

My friend Rich Cobb uses Precision Laser Craft self-sticking shingles on just about all the roofs on my scratchbuilt structure. These little devils come in packages of peel-and-stick strips in a multitude of colors and styles.

Although these shingles look great out of the box or bag, when they're used on a large structure, the monotone color of the roof becomes boring. To remedy this, use a tip from Bob VanGelder, founder of South River Model Works. He suggests using markers of assorted colors to high-light individual shingles to make the roof more visually interesting.

I use markers made by Prismcolor, of Stamford, Connecticut. The colors I have on hand are nos. PM-62 Sepia, PM-69 Goldenrod, PM-80 Putty, PM-102 Warm Gray, and PM-111 Cool Gray.

Each marker has one broad end and one fine end. I use the fine end to color the shingles. Figure 3-8 illustrates how I color them at random. Once I'm satisfied with the multi-color effect, I brush on various shades of dry pigments.

Fig. 3-8: I use Prismcolor markers to add color and visual interest to the Precision Laser Craft shingles.

Fig. 3-4: The pipe that carried the beaming dust out of the building is visible here.

REFERENCES

Hambourg, Serge. *Mills and Factories of New England* (Harry N. Abrams Inc.).

McMartin, Barbara. *The Glove Industries* (Lakeview Press).

Nehrich, John. *Guide to Clothing Manufacturing.* http://railroad.union.rpi.edu/images /Industries/Clothing.asp

HOME TO JOHNSTOWN

Let's take Peerless as an example of the kind of research needed to build a convincing model. I wanted to know why there were so many drums of various sizes scattered around outside the mill and what they would have contained.

Johnstown, where the actual tannery stood, is located in Fulton County, New York. So I began by calling the Fulton County Chamber of Commerce. I was hoping someone there could recommend a contact, someone who knew about the leather industry and might be familiar with history of Peerless.

The folks at the chamber mentioned Barbara McMartin, who had written two excellent books on the leather industry, with emphasis on Gloversville and Johnstown. They also told me about a bookstore that carried her books, and I ordered a copy of each.

From those books, I learned that when an animal hide is tanned, it's transformed from a raw hide that can rot when it becomes wet into something called "leather." Leather, as I learned, is known to be strong, pliable, and virtually waterproof.

Originally, proximity to the bark of oak and hemlock trees, which contain large amounts of "tannin" (hence the word "tanning" when referring to the industry), governed the locations of mills. However, the introduction of chemical processes such as oil, alum, and chrome tanning during the mid-19th and early 20th centuries eventually negated the use of bark.

There are a number of steps in the tanning process. To perform them all, a tanning mill had to be a rather large complex. Through the years, some mills, Peerless Tanning among them, performed only the key steps in that process.

The chamber of commerce also referred me to Bob Bruce, the shop steward of the Glove Workers Union. My phone conversation with him proved enlightening. According to Bob, by the mid-1950s, Peerless was performing only the beaming, tanning, and coloring phases of what's known as the chrome method of leather production. Beaming is the shaving of leather to different thicknesses by special machines equipped with blades or sanding discs. This explains the corrugated metal addition on the back of the building.

Figure 3-4 reveals a pipe running out the rear window of the main building and into that structure. Beaming created a lot of dust, which was drawn through the pipe by fans and deposited into large bags. When full, the bags were removed and disposed of.

The large smokestack to the left of the dust collector served the building's boiler room. The boiler room provided heat for both the building and the large volumes of water that were necessary to complete the different steps of the production process.

While we're on the subject of water, you won't see a millpond or stream in the immediate vicinity of the mill. Peerless used city water, which was piped into the building (by the city water main) and out (most likely through the sewer system).

Bob also shed light on what was (most likely) in all those barrels outside the building. The larger ones would have held untreated hides from such places as Ethiopia and South Africa. In the 1950s, they might also have arrived in large wood casks.

Other barrels would have contained chrome, lime, sulfuric acid, salt, and dyes. The product emerging from Peerless would have been finished, tanned, and dyed hides of different sizes, colors, and thickness that, in turn, would have been sold and shipped to other manufacturers to be made into jackets, gloves, pocketbooks, shoes, and the like.

Although not apparent in the prototype photos, there would likely have been an array of boxes lying around in which to ship out this finished leather. Note that there are numerous pallets in those photos.

DETAILING THE MODEL

Figure 3-5 shows the details I added around the model. Scale Structures Limited supplied barrels (item no. 650-2017 and -2514), sacks (650-2126 and -2128), boxes (650-2151), two dollies (650-2281), a welding cart and hose (650-2311 and -2312), oil drums (650-2349 and -2463), and pallets (650-2455 and -2501).

A group of Woodland Scenics no. 785-1823 Dock Workers quit the docks, ditched their hardhats, and joined the Glove Workers Union. Now they've come to work at Peerless. Martin Collard's scratch-built stake body Ford awaits loading.

Also compare the prototype shown in fig. 3-6 with the picture of the model in fig. 3-7. Where the north side of the actual building was flanked by a sidewalk (since the mill was off line), I had Rich Cobb alter that facade on the model by adding two freight doors so a rail siding could serve the industry.

As I said in the introduction, no matter what industry you chose to model, you should devote time to research. You'll understand the concept of operation of that industry. In turn, you as a modeler can provide a more realistic representation of it in miniature with the addition of some of the myriad of details available today.

ADDITIONAL STRUCTURE OPTIONS

If you aren't up to scratchbuilding Peerless Tanning Company, here are some commercial options that, with a few alterations or a bit of kitbashing, will fit the bill:

American Model Builders no. 152-2001 Dabler Mill and Supply
SS Limited no. 650-1523 Wischers Washer Company
Walthers Cornerstone no. 933-3069 Front Street Warehouse
Walthers Cornerstone no. 933-3084 Lakeside Shipping
Walthers Cornerstone no. 933-3095 Railway Express Agency

Fig. 3-5: The rear view of the model from the southeast shows how commercial details add to the authenticity of the scene.

Fig. 3-6: Because the prototype mill was "off line," there were no loading doors along the north facade.

Fig. 3-7: Rich Cobb added loading doors on the north wall of the model since it would be served by rail.

BIGGER IS SOMETIMES BETTER

Eager to add more industries to our layouts, modelers often run rail sidings to mills that aren't much larger than one of the freight cars serving them. While there are cases of this happening in real life, it generally doesn't look convincing on a model railroad.

We do this because we worry about space limitations. However, you may be surprised as to just how large a structure you can fit into a supposedly limited space.

Let's take a look at a location on my HO scale West Hoosic Division layout as an example. In figs. 3-9 and 3-10, taken in the early 1980s, we see my original Smith/Elwell Machine Company with a siding to it. This factory represented a kitbash of two Tyco interlocking towers—an interesting structure but hardly one warranting its own siding.

Figures 3-11 and 3-12, taken 16 years later, show the building that replaced the original. We're still looking at the same amount

of real estate, about 8 by 19 inches, but now we have a more substantial structure, one that could warrant its own rail siding.

Although this mill is scratchbuilt, it wouldn't be difficult to kitbash one or more of the fine commercial buildings available today into a similar complex.

Figs. 3-9 and 3-10: The original Smith / Elwell Mill on the HO scale West Hoosic Division was a kitbash of two Tyco interlocking towers. It seemed too small to warrant its own siding.

Figs. 3-11 and 3-12: Rich Cobb scratchbuilt a new structure that nicely fills the available real estate.

The street w

While preparing the previous chapter, I decided to create a model scene based on what's near the actual Peerless Tanning mill. Since this would include about a one-block area, my wife and I decided a field trip back to Peerless was in order.

As we wandered around—notebook, tape measure, and camera in hand—we realized that the streets around Peerless, like most urban byways, offered myriad details that should be present on a model.

The tractor-trailer moving by Peerless Tanning Company doesn't draw nearly as much attention from the locals as action on the railroad would.

here you live

A BRIEF HISTORY

Let's first discuss the details we might find on a typical 1950s urban street (see fig. 4-1). The thoroughfare would be paved with concrete or blacktop. The latter was the material of choice in regions subjected to heavy snow and ice because concrete doesn't stand up to the heavy use of salt.

In an older section of a city— like that around Peerless, which was probably originally developed in the early 19th century—there would be curbing of some sort, most likely granite, slate, or marble slabs. Concrete and blacktop curbing began to replace solid stone to a large extent by the middle of the 20th century.

In the 1970s, machines were developed that laid a continuous strip of concrete or blacktop curbing. Technology thus negated the necessity of sectional construction and the inherent manual labor that was involved.

Additional details would include manhole covers, usually situated in the center of the roadway, to provide access to the sanitary sewers. Catch basins along the edge of the

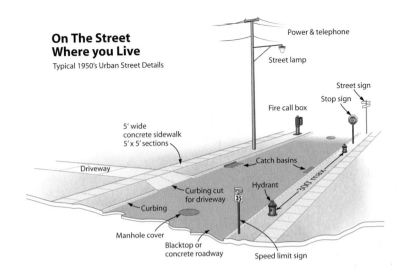

On The Street Where you Live
Typical 1950's Urban Street Details

Power & telephone
Street lamp
Street sign
Stop sign
Fire call box
5' wide concrete sidewalk 5' x 5' sections
Catch basins
Driveway
Curbing cut for driveway
Hydrant
Speed limit 35
Curbing
Manhole cover
Blacktop or concrete roadway
Speed limit sign

Fig. 4-1: Here are the components of a typical urban street scene.

pavement, butted against the curbing, would provide drainage.

Fire hydrants and fire department call boxes would be in evidence along the sides of the street. Both had to be easily accessible in the event of a fire.

Streetlights were also likely to be present. Many times they were mounted on the same poles that carried the power and telephone lines to residences and businesses.

Street signs would be located at each corner so people could identify the byways. Speed limit, stop, and yield signs would be used to control vehicular traffic.

In cities, as opposed to rural settings, mailboxes were mounted on the front of the houses. Or they might be nothing more than a slot in or near a front door since the high density of homes made door-to-door mail service more feasible.

A WORKING CLASS NEIGHBORHOOD

Urban thoroughfares exist to provide access and services to the residences and businesses on them. Since the town of Johnstown was, and still is to some extent, a mill town, I decided to add a series of company houses opposite Peerless.

What are company houses? Back in the good old days, mill owners built houses and rented them to their workers so they could provide

them with housing and also make a few extra bucks.

These houses tended to be modestly appointed buildings, utilitarian in design. Most were built to the same specifications and had the same basic amenities. Hence, they all looked alike. Occasionally, they were built as a series of apartments, all in one structure, but in our model they are separate dwellings.

By the mid-1940s, companies were divesting themselves of the houses because they were going out of business or they wanted to get them and their inherent maintenance costs off the books. Once the occupants became homeowners rather than tenants, they began to alter and improve their abodes.

MODELING THE SCENE

Since I discussed the prototype scene from the ground up, let me explain how I tackled the model in the same order. I planned my scene to be from the mid-1950s; if you select a later era, be sure to substitute updated details if necessary.

I chose to replicate blacktop pavement, concrete sidewalks, and driveways with a Scale Crete from CS Design (item no. 155-7001). I've used it to create the look of concrete and blacktop roads with excellent results, as described in my previous books.

Scale Crete has many of the properties of real concrete, though it's much finer in texture. It comes in a premixed 32-ounce package.

I included the usual signs of underground utilities that would be present in a roadway, such as storm sewer catch basins and sanitary sewer manhole covers. For catch basins and manhole covers I turned to SS Limited, which markets HO scale versions of both (nos. 650-2334 and 650-2333, respectively).

My streets needed curbs. I relied on Evergreen Scale Models no. 269-164 .080 x .080-inch styrene strips for this application.

For fire protection, I decided on SS Limited nos. 650-2491 fireplugs and 650-2336 fire call boxes. I opted for Blair Line nos. 184-109 street signs, 184-102 regulatory signs, 184-143 vintage warning signs, and 184-107 warning signs. Creative Model Associates no. 363-1009 cross bucks were also used.

Rix poles carry power, telephone service, and street lighting. These come in two parts, the main pole and a choice of cross arms. I went with nos. 628-40 40-foot poles and 628-35 clear (actually, a realistic emerald green) cross arms. (I'll have more to say about pole lines and the details that go along with them in the next chapter.)

For the company houses on our street, I used six (seven, if you count the two-story addition on the corner house) of City Classics no. 195-111 Railroad Street Company Houses. Rich Cobb modified them as though they had been in private ownership for a few years by making additions and improvements.

WATCH YOUR BACK

When creating an urban scene, bear in mind that backyards can be as interesting as front yards In back of each house I added garbage cans from SS Limited (nos. 650-2421, 2429, and 2430) and On Trak Model Products (no. 786-645). Two Preiser no. 590-10463 gardeners work on their garden, and a derelict Jordan Products no. 360-225 1940 Ford sedan rusts away on blocks in the driveway next door.

Every neighborhood has a family or two that let its property go to the dogs. That's a Woodland Scenics no. 785-1814 dog barking out back. Alongside the garage we see an SS Limited nos. 650-5111 wringer washer and 650-5153 claw-leg bathtub, a Preiser no. 590-10333 bicycle, and assorted barrels and boxes.

The yards are separated by a variety of Central Valley no. 210-1601 fences. At least three homes get TV reception through Gold Medal Models no. 304-8705 antennas.

The backyard near Peerless Tanning is a fascinating world.

STARTING CONSTRUCTION

Let's begin by laying asphalt, adding curbing, and installing the manhole covers and catch basins. Figure 4-2 depicts the details used; fig. 4-3 shows the tools and materials.

After drawing the edge of the roadway on the base (25 scale feet wide in this case) in pencil, I laid seven layers of masking tape on each edge, as fig. 4-4 shows. This created forms between which I spread the blacktop material.

Next, I glued the catch basins in place with Weld Bond. Using an artist's spatula, I spread Scale Crete over the scenery base (fig. 4-5), working the material around the edge of the catch basins.

I used a 4-inch-wide putty knife to span the masking tape on each side of the pavement and drew the knife slowly along the length of the road to smooth out the Scale Crete (fig. 4-6). Once I was satisfied with the smoothness of the surface, I ran a hobby knife with an X-acto no 11 blade along the edge of the Scale Crete (fig. 4-7) and gently peeled away the masking tape (fig. 4-8).

Don't get too worried if the roadway is not exceptionally smooth, especially around the catch basins. After the material has set for about 15 minutes, you can gently tap the surface with your finger and remove any irregularities.

My advice is to not wait too long to do this. Once the Scale Crete has dried, it lives up to its name and becomes as hard as . . . you guessed it . . . concrete!

While waiting 2 to 3 hours for the Scale Crete to dry, I used my hobby knife to notch out the strip styrene curbing at 4 scale foot intervals. I gave the strips a first coat of Polly Scale no. 270-414116 Reefer Gray.

Then I installed the curbing by applying tube-type styrene cement (fig. 4-9) to attach the strips to the road surface (fig. 4-10). When you do this, leave curb cuts where you want to locate driveways (see fig. 4-1).

I installed manhole covers by drilling a hole in the road surface with a ⁵⁄₁₆ inch bit (fig. 4-11). The covers were slightly larger than the hole, so I opened up the hole with an X-acto no. 11 blade (fig. 4-12). After trial-fitting the covers, I applied a drop of Weld Bond to the bottom of each and pressed them in place (fig. 4-13).

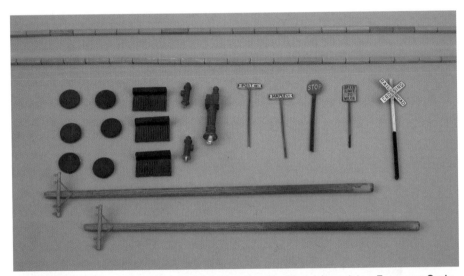

Fig. 4-2: The author used details from Blair Line, Creative Model Associates, Evergreen Scale Models, Rix Power Plus Products, and SS Limited to model his street scene.

Fig. 4-3: Necessary tools and materials include a power drill with a ⁵⁄₁₆ inch bit; Woodland Scenics plaster cloth; India ink/rubbing alcohol wash; CS Design Scale Crete; masking tape; Testor's plastic cement; Polly Scale Concrete, Grimy Black, and Reefer Gray paints; Weld Bond glue; a putty knife; an X-acto hobby knife and blade; artist's spatula; small paintbrushes; and Weber-Costello dry pigments.

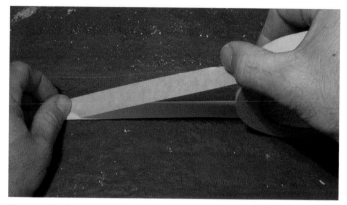

Fig. 4-4: First apply about seven layers of masking tape the width of the road apart.

Fig. 4-5: After gluing the catch basins, spread the Scale Crete with an artist's spatula.

Fig. 4-6: Smooth out the Scale Crete with a putty knife.

Fig. 4-7: Use a hobby knife with an X-acto no. 11 blade to cut the edges of the Scale Crete along the tape.

Fig 4-8: Peel the tape away from the surface.

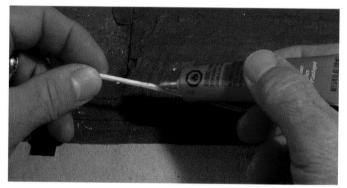

Fig. 4-9: Apply plastic cement to the edge of the curbing.

Fig. 4-10: Press the curbing into place.

Fig 4-11: Using a 5⁄16" bit, drill holes for the manhole covers.

Fig 4-12: Ream out the edges of the holes with a no. 11 X-acto hobby knife.

Fig. 4-13: Dab Weld Bond onto the bottom of the manhole cover and press it in place.

THE SIDEWALKS

I also used Scale Crete to create the sidewalks on the module. I opted for the look of 5-foot-square concrete sections. There's a 5-foot-wide green area between the sidewalks and roadways around Peerless.

To create this effect, I applied about five layers of Woodland Scenics plaster cloth along each side of the pavement about 5 feet from the curbing (fig. 4-14). This brought the base of the sidewalk up to the top of the curbing (fig. 4-15). Once the gauze had dried, I painted it with the earth tone paint I used on the rest of the base (fig. 4-16).

Like the roadway, the sidewalk is built by spreading Scale Crete between (seven-layered) masking-tape forms. Since I wanted the walk to look like it was poured in 5-foot-square sections, I marked the masking tape on both sides of the walk at 5-foot intervals in pencil (fig. 4-17). This helped me align the seams in the walk.

Next, I spread the Scale Crete between the masking tape and ran an X-acto no. 11 blade along each edge. Using the pencil marks as a guide, I cut in the seams between each section (fig. 4-18).

I then removed the tape and gave the walks about 15 minutes to dry. I finished by scribing in cracks at random with my hobby knife.

Fig. 4-14: Apply seven layers of plaster cloth where you want your sidewalk to be located.

Fig. 4-16: Paint the gauze with earth-colored paint.

Fig. 4-15: Creating a green area between the roadway and sidewalk requires building up the scenery base beneath the walk with plaster cloth to raise the elevation of the walk to match the top of the curbing.

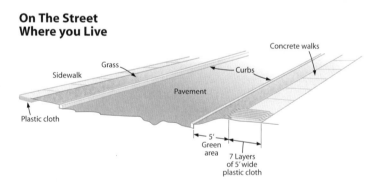
On The Street Where you Live

Fig. 4-17: After applying seven layers of masking tape, mark the tape on each side of the seams in the sidewalk.

Fig. 4-18: Scribe the sidewalk seams using the pencil lines on the tape as a guide.

FINISHING UP

Next, I brush-painted the road with full-strength Polly Scale no. 270-414137 Grimy Black (fig. 4-19). I then added a second coat of Reefer Gray to the curbing (fig. 4-20).

After the walks dried, I brush-painted them with Polly Scale no. 270-414317 Concrete (fig. 4-21). I highlighted the seams between the walk sections by applying a mix of India ink and rubbing alcohol (1 teaspoon ink to 1 pint alcohol).

Using a small soft bristle brush, I weathered the pavement, curbs, and walks by dry-brushing on Weber-Costello dry pigments (see fig. 4-22).

After applying ground cover to the area between the roadway and walks, I added fireplugs and call boxes. Hydrants can be no more than 300 feet apart in our town. I placed call boxes at intersections, so they can serve a four-block area.

To keep my Preiser people from getting lost, speeding, or crashing, I installed Blair Line traffic and street signs. I used Creative Model Associates cross bucks to protect the railroad crossings, and Rix poles to bring power and telephone service to the neighborhood.

Fig. 4-19: Paint the roadway with full-strength Polly Scale Grimy Black.

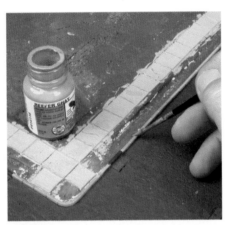

Fig. 4-20: Paint the curbing with Polly Scale Reefer Gray.

Fig. 4-21: Paint the sidewalk with Polly Scale Concrete.

Fig. 4-22: Weather the roadway, curbs, and sidewalks with an application of shades of Weber-Costello dry gray pigment.

HOUSING FOR THE MASSES

I decided to use City Classics company houses for this project. Let's take a look at how to vary their appearance. Keep in mind these houses have, in theory, been sold by the company and are now being improved by their owners.

Let's take the two houses in figs. 4-23 and 4-24 as examples. The house on the right is an out-of-the-box model, while the house on the left has had some improvements, including a fresh coat of paint.

I enclosed the porch using Evergreen Scale Models no. 269-2040 scribed siding and Grandt Line no. 300-5022 and 300-5029 windows, 300-5064 lattices, and 300-5058 doors. I modified the rather plain roof with Precision Laser Craft no. 2345 dark gray self-sticking asbestos shingles. As the photos illustrate, a little bit of creative work yields a different look.

Fig. 4-23: Front view of "before and after" mill house detailing. The Precision Laser Craft shingles and enclosed porch add interest and character to the structure.

Fig. 4-24: Rear three-quarter view of "before and after" mill houses.

MATERIALS

Streets

Blair Line no. 184-102 regulatory signs
Blair Line no. 184-107 warning signs
Blair Line no. 184-109 street signs
Blair Line no. 184-143 vintage warning signs
Creative Model Associates no. 363-1009 cross bucks
CS Design no. 155-7001 Scale Crete
Evergreen Scale Models no. 269-164 .080" x .080" styrene strip
Rix Power Plus Products no. 628-35 emerald green cross arms
Rix Power Plus Products no. 628-40 40-foot power poles
SS Limited no. 650-2333 manhole covers
SS Limited no. 650-2334 catch basins
SS Limited no. 650-2336 fire call boxes
SS Limited no. 650-2491 fire plugs

Houses

City Classics no. 195-111 Railroad Street Company Houses
Evergreen Scale Models no. 269-2040 scribed siding
Grandt Line no. 300-5022
Grandt Line no. 300-5029 windows
Grandt Line no. 300-5058 doors
Grandt Line no. 300-5064 lattices
Precision Laser Craft no. 2345 gray self-sticking asbestos shingles

Yards

Central Valley no. 210-1601 fences
Gold Medal Models no. 304-8705 television antennas

Jordan Products no. 360-225 Ford sedan
Preiser no. 10333 bicycles
SS Limited no. 650-2421 open garbage cans
SS Limited no. 650-2429 open garbage cans
SS Limited no. 650-2430 garbage cans
SS Limited no. 650-5153 claw-leg bathtub
SS Limited no. 650-5111 wringer washer

Figures

Preiser no. 590-80904 Z scale figures
Preiser no. 590-79127 N scale figures
Woodland Scenics no. 785-1814 family with dog

HOW TO BEND PLASTIC CURBING

By now you are probably asking, "Styrene might make good curbing but how do I bend it around the corners at street intersections?" Let me offer a great technique.

Begin by laying the styrene strips over a section of ⅝" diameter brass tubing while heating the plastic with a hairdryer. When the styrene heats up, it becomes flexible and can be bent around the tubing to form a tight radius. (fig. 4-25).

Fig. 4-25: Use a hair dryer and brass tubing to bend the plastic curbing to the desired shape.

CREATING A UNIQUE FIGURE

One detail that reeks of the 1950s is the "Bathtub Madonna." Just about anyone who was replacing an old claw-leg bathtub with a "built-in" variety decided to pay homage to Mary by placing her in a discarded bathtub, usually on the front lawn.

John Nehrich describes modeling this scene in HO scale in the May 2001 issue of *Model Railroader.* I followed his suggestions, but substituted an SS Limited no. 650-5153 claw-leg bathtub. I used a Z scale figure (Preiser no. 590-80904) as seen in figs. 4-26 and 4-27; an N scale one would also work (the nun in Preiser no. 590-79127).

Fig. 4-26: The Z scale Arab figure I used for my "Bathtub Madonna."

Fig. 4-27: With his robes repainted, our Z scale Arab poses as Mary on the corner of Fulton and Spruce Streets.

Milkin' the

Adding a facility to ship milk, cream, and other dairy products to your HO layout can be a lot of fun, and it will certainly catch the eye of every viewer. But as always, doing adequate research is necessary before you start construction.

To determine what's involved with the shipment of milk by rail, let's first turn to the website maintained by the Rensselaer Model Railroad Society for its famed HO layout, the New England, Berkshire & Western.

Rutland Ten-Wheeler no. 74 passes the Grand Isle Creamery as it heads south on the main line to Burlington.

DAIRY SHIPPING FACILITIES

Information on creameries on the Rutland Railroad line can be found on the NEB&W Web site. The following is an excerpt:

"The facilities for shipping out milk by rail can be divided into three types. The simplest were small platforms, which may or may not have had a roof. These were located next to the main line, without a separate siding, as cans were loaded into milk cars while they were still coupled to the train.

"If greater traffic warranted, milk companies would build a receiving station, often in connection with an icehouse. These milk stations rarely had their own siding either, as loading could still be accomplished directly onto the train while it waited.

"Most photos show these buildings to be two-story wood frame structures, usually painted gray with white trim. They often sat back far from the track, with a long platform extending out to the rails. Farmers could use the dock to load directly onto the train without passing through the building.

"Bulk milk facilities came into their own around 1925 to 1930. These were complete processing units, including pasteurization, and in some cases probably using mechanical refrigeration to chill the milk rather than using the ice cut from ponds the previous winter.

"In most cases these had their own siding, where a milk tank car could be set out the day before. These sidings stand out on track maps as being double-ended for speed of switching, but often very short, just a car length or two.

"In rare cases if the volume shipped was less than a whole car, two creameries in different towns would share one milk car. The train would pick up a partially loaded car at the first creamery, and further down the line wait while the car would be filled at the second. Bulk milk creameries also could and did ship the product in cans.

"Creameries tended to be constructed out of cheaper wood or cinder blocks; brick was rarely used. The buildings typically had two stories and often with a gambrel roof (with dormers) in an apparent attempt to emulate a dairy barn.

"Creameries, especially those made of wood, usually sprawled. That is, they had several one-story additions. In addition, tall smokestacks, large roof ventilators, and elevated industrial-type water towers were common.

"Nearly every creamery boasted a small 'can' door, just large enough to pass cans into the building from a farmer's wagon or truck. Opening such a small door instead of a normal-sized one cut down on air circulation and loss of cool air from inside, which was particularly important in the days of primitive refrigeration.

"The presence of an icehouse indicated that natural ice was being used. The icehouse was a large, windowless building, either adjacent to the complex or attached at one end. The icehouse was often the larger portion of the whole creamery complex."

Milk operations along a right-of-way can range from a simple baggage car (milk-can load) to a sprawling complex (mixed-construction) of structures. This diversity offers advantages to modelers confronted with space limitations, as does the relative simplicity of construction methods of even larger complexes.

A DIVERSITY OF STYLES

Creameries of Upstate New York by John W. Hudson provides insights into the various architectural styles used in creamery construction. Let's look at several of the vintage photos contained in that book.

Figure 5-1, taken on April 20, 1908, shows the Boston Creamery on the Buffalo & Susquehanna Railroad. This Boston, by the way, is a small town in western New York. In later years pickups and flatbed trucks replaced the horses and buggies.

Figure 5-2 shows the off-line Clove Valley creamery, which looked more like a two-and-a-half-story farmhouse than a creamery. (You could easily kitbash a couple of City Classics row houses to replicate this structure.

Figure 5-3 depicts the Fernwood, creamery on the New York Central line in upstate New York. Note the milk cans stacked on the platform awaiting the arrival of their intended milk car. The three men on the platform have more heavy lifting ahead.

None of these three structures was overwhelming in size, yet all warranted the rail traffic. Best of all, any of them could be modeled with relative ease.

Fig. 5-1: The grand opening of the Boston Creamery on the Buffalo & Susquehanna Railroad's Buffalo Division on April 20, 1908. Courtesy Collection of Depot Square Publishing

Fig. 5-2: The Clove Valley Creamery was off line and looks more like a typical two-and-a-half-story farmhouse of the period than an operating creamery. A model of this structure would make an interesting conversation piece. Courtesy Collection of Depot Square Publishing

Fig. 5-3: The Fernwood, New York, Creamery on the New York Central's Syracuse & Massena Springs Line. Three workers have just stacked the cans on the platform and pause to enjoy a glimpse of some ladies as they await the arrival of the milk train. Courtesy Collection of Depot Square Publishing

FROM PROTOTYPE TO MODEL

Now that we've looked at some prototype creameries, let's look at some models. Jack Wright is the owner of the Schoharie Valley Railroad, an HO scale layout that was featured in the 1999 issue of *Great Model Railroads*.

Jack decided to put two scratch-built creameries on his line. One is the Sheffield Farm Creamery in the town of Schoharie Center (fig. 5-4). The other is the Dairyman's League Plant in Fox Creek (fig. 5-5).

STRUCTURE OPTIONS FOR A CREAMERY

Campbell Scale Models no. 200-418 Farmers Co-op Creamery

South River Millett Creamery (out of production)

Walthers Cornerstone no. 933-3061 Sunrise Feedmill

Fig. 5-4: Jack Wright's HO scale Schoharie Valley Railroad sports not one, but two scratchbuilt creameries. The one pictured here, in Schoharie Center, is owned by Sheffield Farms.

Fig. 5-5: Jack's other creamery is the Dairyman's League plant in Fox Creek, which is modeled after a prototype creamery on the Rutland Railroad.

Fig. 5-6: A worker checks the temperature of incoming milk to make sure it meets standards. Courtesy *New York, Ontario & Western Railway Milk Cans, Mixed Trains and Motorcars* by Robert E. Mohowski

AN INSIDE JOB

So much for the exterior of the creameries, but what actually went on inside a typical creamery? For answers, we need to consult *New York Ontario & Western Railway Milk Cans, Mixed Trains, and Motorcars* by Bob Mohowski.

This book states that collection points for milk were called creameries, milk receiving stations, shipping depots, or milk plants. They could be owned and operated by local people, a farmers' cooperative, or a large dairy company such as Borden's or the Dairymen's League.

"The best location for a creamery was near an ample supply of good water and a large number of cows (to ensure an adequate supply of milk). It also had to have adequate drainage for disposal of wastewater.

"Work at a typical creamery began well before dawn. The furnace grates had to be shaken, and a layer of coal needed to be spread over the fire. Steam and hot water were needed for cleaning milk cans, holding tanks, pipes, and fittings through which the milk would pass.

"Farmers started arriving not long after sunrise. An efficient creamery was usually arranged so that the milk cans came in one side of the building and processed city-bound milk went out the other.

"Raw milk arriving from farms, in separate evening and morning cans, was placed on a conveyor of rollers that ran along an outside wall. It then entered the creamery by way of a small door that was slightly taller than the height of the cans.

"Workers subjected each can to a number of tests and procedures to determine the quality and quantity of the raw milk. Temperature and sediment checks were done first (fig. 5-6), and then the milk was filtered to remove hair, dust, and other impurities. It then headed to a weighing tank (fig. 5-7).

"At some point samples were taken and checked in a small lab for butterfat content and bacteria count. The milk then left the weighing tank and entered a cooling system.

"Cooling was done—before rural electrification became widespread—by pouring the milk into clean cans submersed in ice-water vats or tanks. By the 1920s, some creameries had converted to electrical appliances and cooling systems.

"Many facilities had a cream separator that removed the cream from the raw milk. Some cream was later added to milk that was sold for regular consumption. Other dairy products that originated at creameries were butter, buttermilk, cheese, evaporated and skim milk, ice cream, and sour cream.

"After being emptied the cans continued along the conveyor to a can-washing station. Once the cans had been dried, their lids were attached (fig. 5-8). Then the cans passed out of the building via another conveyor, where the owner claimed them by the letters and/or numbers he had applied (fig. 5-9)."

Fig. 5-7: Milk is poured into a weighing tank. The cans will be put through the washer on the left. Courtesy *New York, Ontario & Western Railway Milk Cans, Mixed Trains and Motorcars* by Robert E. Mohowski

Fig. 5-8: The cans and lids are matched after passing through the washer and dryer. Courtesy *New York, Ontario & Western Railway Milk Cans, Mixed Trains and Motorcars* by Robert E. Mohowski

Fig. 5-9: A farmer loads his clean cans at a creamery in Owego, New York. The elapsed time from delivery to departure was about 15 minutes. Courtesy *New York, Ontario & Western Railway Milk Cans, Mixed Trains and Motorcars* by Robert E. Mohowski

THE CREAMERY AT GRAND ISLE

With all this information at hand, plus the illustration of a typical creamery (fig. 5-10), we're ready to begin work on the creamery I decided to replicate. It's a structure on the NEB&W known as the creamery at Grand Isle.

In reality, this model is based on a creamery once found on the Rutland Railroad's main line between Burlington and Alburgh, Vermont. Figure 5-11 shows that complex prior to 1929.

While Rich Cobb built the structure, I prepared the module it would be located on. Since this was most likely a creamery that handled bulk and individual canned product, I opted for a double-ended siding approximately 200 feet long.

Let's take a look at the model and see how it captures some of the details I described earlier in this chapter. In fig. 5-12, we see the icehouse, a large structure without windows attached on the north end of the complex.

The icehouse has five doors running up the center of the north end of the structure. These would be opened individually for loading and stacking of blocks of ice.

The small shed on the platform

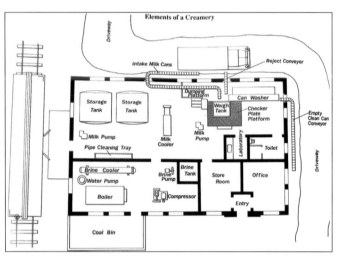

Fig. 5-10: This diagram shows the various elements of a creamery.

Fig. 5-11: The Grand Isle County Co-op looking south. Courtesy *The Rutland—Sixty Years of Trying* by Robert W. Nimke

Fig. 5-12: Here we see the north end of the creamery at Grand Isle. The series of doors in the center of the end wall are used for storing block ice obtained from a nearby pond during the cold winter months.

These doors can be opened individually as the ice is piled higher inside the structure.

in fig. 5-13 would most likely provide a shelter for creamery employees working the loading dock in adverse weather. Here they could do whatever paperwork was necessary without being at the mercy of the elements. The length of the platform would allow creamery employees and train crews to stack large quantities of full cans for loading and returning empty cans for pickup.

Figure 5-14 shows the south end of the building. To the left of the entrance door are the conveyor and the small milk-loading door. Full cans would be placed on the conveyor and passed through the small door into the building. In fig. 5-15, the shorter conveyor on the west side is for rejected cans; the one to the left is the empty can return.

The large smokestack in fig. 5-16 serves the furnace and boiler. These heat the structure while providing heat for milk pasteurization, along with steam and hot water for the sterilization and cleaning of the vats and cans used for storage and transport of the product.

Fig. 5-13: The small structure on the platform provides shelter for creamery and railroad workers as they wait for the necessary paperwork—for the loading and unloading—to be completed.

Fig. 5-14: The south end view of the building has the conveyor and small milk-loading door to the left of the larger entry door.

Fig. 5-15: This view of the west side of the model shows the shorter conveyor on the right that would hold rejected cans while the conveyor to the left is the empty can return.

Fig. 5-16: The large smokestack serves the furnace and boiler that heat the structure and provide heat for milk pasteurization as well as steam and hot water for sterilization and the cleaning of vats and cans used for storing and transporting of the product.

TYPES OF MILK CARS

Next, we need to direct our attention to the types of railroad cars that would serve such an industry. One, the privately owned milk car, carried the product in bulk. The other type of car, owned by a railroad, carried individual milk cans.

Pfaudler was one of the primary suppliers of bulk cars. A number of 40- and 50-foot-long styles of Pfaudler cars plied the rails over the years.

The construction of most of these cars consisted of a wood or steel outer body enclosing two large glass-lined containers in which milk was stored during shipment. Earlier versions had a removable roof.

Figure 5-17 shows an early car with four lift rings, two along the upper edge of each side of the roof, where a crane's hook could be attached to lift the roof off the car. The removable roof allowed access to the containers if repair or replacement was needed (fig. 5-18).

As the years passed and the interior containers proved to be reliable, the lift rings and removable roofs were eliminated (fig. 5-19). All milk cars had a set of tightly sealing double doors on each side through which a person could pass.

There would also be a small sliding access door above those double doors. A hose could slide through this opening and into the car to allow milk to flow directly to the interior tanks from the storage tanks in the creamery.

Because the car's tanks were insulated (though the cars were not refrigerated), using these small sliding doors allowed the loading crew to keep the larger doors closed. This helped keep warm outside air from entering the car during the loading process.

Figure 5-20 shows a railroad-owned milk car (a Boston & Maine model built by Jack Wright). Unlike the Pfaudler car, it doesn't have glass-lined tanks on the interior. Instead, individual milk cans were loaded and shipped on this type of car. As a result, there are no small, sliding doors above the sealed larger doors on each side of the car.

SCRATCHBUILDING A MILK CAN CONVEYOR

Lacking any commercial HO milk-can conveyors, Rich Cobb came up with the ingenious idea of cutting round toothpicks to the required length and gluing them together to form rollers. He added cardstock sides, plastic angle stock legs, and more scrap cardstock for the leg cross braces.

Rich painted the assembly with Floquil no. 270-110100 Old Silver to create a convincing model (below). The completed assembly and its components are shown at right.

Incoming milk cans have been placed on Rich Cobb's scratchbuilt steel roller conveyor and are ready to enter the building.

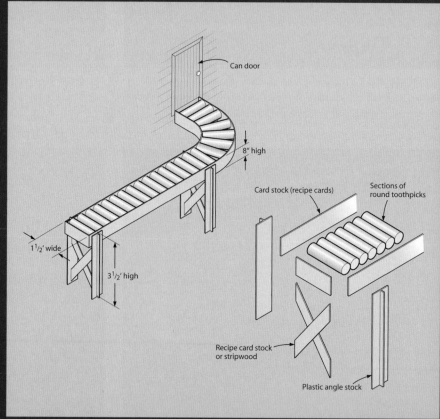

Here we see the typical conveyor in both assembled form and broken down into its components. The dimensions are approximate.

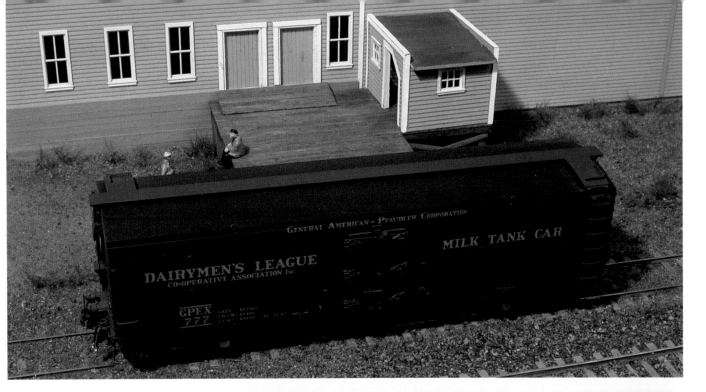

Fig. 5-17: An Overland HO brass model from the 1980s of an early wood-sided Pfaudler car reveals the removable roof with four lift rings, two on each side. By attaching a hook to each of these rings a crane could lift the roof off the car, allowing access to the large storage cylinders. These cars were built in 40- and 50-foot lengths.

Fig. 5-18: This photo shows a Pfaudler car under construction at the firm's East Chicago shops. The holding tanks are in place in the car but have yet to be wrapped in insulation. Courtesy *New York, Ontario & Western Railway Milk Cans, Mixed Trains and Motorcars* by Robert E. Mohowski.

Fig. 5-19: Here we see an Overland version of a later Pfaudler car. The car's exterior was all steel, and the roof is permanent. Note that this particular car has a straight sill. Cars similar in appearance were built with rolled or curved bottom sills. These cars could also be 40 or 50 feet long.

Fig. 5-20: Jack Wright built this resin model of a Boston & Maine milk car. This type of car didn't have glass-lined storage tanks installed. Instead, milk was transported in individual cans, which eliminated the need for the small sliding access doors, or panels, above the larger doors on the sides of these cars.

There were also a number of other styles of cars in use through the period. Two worth mentioning are the Borden's "butter dish" car and the tanker truck trailer car.

The butter dish car (fig. 5-21) was so called because of its uncanny resemblance to a dish that people used on their dining-room tables. The tanker truck trailer car was a specially designed flatcar with a swiveling mechanism that held two tanker trailers (see figs. 5-22 and 5-23). The trailers were loaded directly onto their respective flatcar at a siding, thus making a couple of truck cabs and a loading ramp one of the least complicated industries you'll ever model.

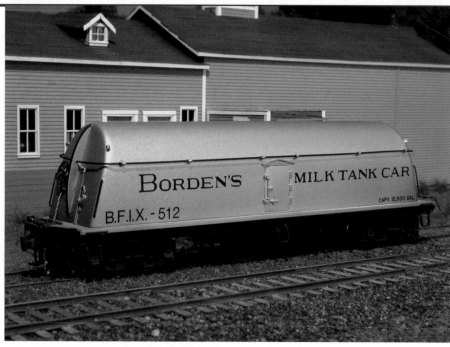

Fig. 5-21: Here we have a Borden's "butterdish" car, so named because of its resemblance to the common butterdish that sat on many dining-room tables.

MATERIALS

Details West
   235-922 2-bolt fishplates
Evergreen Hill Designs
   261 EH-659 milk cans
Micro Engineering
   10-106 code 70 flextrack
   10-108 code 55 flextrack
   14-805 code 70 left-hand turnout
   14-806 code 70 right-hand turnout
   26-055 code 55 rail joiners
   26-070 code 70 rail joiners
On Trak Model Products
   786-602 milk cans
Woodland Scenics
   785-1447 Subterrain Foam Putty

REFERENCES

Hudson, John W. *Creameries of Upstate New York At the Turn of the Century*: (Robert A. Liljestrand).

Mohowski, Robert E. *New York Ontario & Western Railway Milk Cans, Mixed Trains, and Motorcars* (Garrigues House).

Nimke, Robert W. *The Rutland—Sixty Years of Trying* (Sharp Offset Printing).

Liljestrand, Robert A., and Nehrich, John. *Railway Milk Cars, Vol. 1* (Bob's Photo).

Fig. 5-22 and Fig. 5-23: This Overland model captures the look of a twin tanker milk car. The actual car necessitated the use of a ramp or platform next to the track for loading and unloading by truck. The trailers were backed onto the car and swiveled into position.

SUPERDETAILING FLEXTRACK

Not too long ago, about the only way to create realistic trackwork with scale rail was to lay individual ties, stain and weather them, and then spike code 83, 70, 55, or 40 nickel-silver rail to them. Now, however, several manufacturers offer finely detailed nickel-silver flextrack in a variety of rail sizes. When correctly weathered, they can look more realistic than hand-laid track.

Micro Engineering produces a line of realistic code 83, code 70, and code 55 flextrack. Each tie has cast-on tie plates and four scale spikes per rail, per plate. Micro Engineering also makes an assortment of finely detailed turnouts.

As nicely detailed as these items are, modelers can easily make them better. Let me show you what I did on my Grand Isle Creamery module.

I chose code 70 rail for the mainline track. Because sidings and yard trackage are usually subject to less high-speed traffic, I generally use code 40 or, in this case, code 55. Industrial sidings are often slightly lower than the main line since ballasting, weed control, and tie maintenance aren't as important.

For the creamery I used Homabed roadbed for both the mainline and the siding (fig. 5-24). The mainline roadbed is about ¼" thick, while the siding roadbed is ⅛" thick (fig. 5-26). This variation in thickness allowed me to make the siding elevation about one scale foot lower than the mainline track.

I used Woodland Scenics no. 785-1447 Subterrain Foam Putty to blend the lower elevation of the siding with that of the main line. After spreading the putty with a knife (fig. 5-27), I used a sanding block to smooth out the surface (fig. 5-28).

To attach the code 55 rail to the code 70 turnouts, I installed a rail joiner on the code 70 rail and then crushed the exposed end. I soldered the code 55 to the top of the rail joiner (fig. 5-29).

Next, I installed Details West no. 235-922 2-bolt fishplates along the outside of each rail every 39 feet. After first trimming off the spikes at each tie (fig. 5-30), I used epoxy to glue the fishplates in place (fig. 5-31).

Next I painted the track with an inexpensive aerosol gray primer (fig. 5-32). I brush-painted the sides of the rails with Floquil no. 270-110007 Rail Brown (fig. 5-33). Finally, I applied a wash of India ink and rubbing alcohol (1 teaspoon India ink to 1 pint alcohol), then cleaned the railheads between each step with a Bright Boy (fig. 5-34).

Once I'd done the ballasting, it was difficult to tell the difference between our HO track and the real thing.

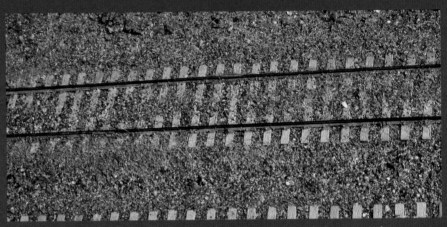

Fig. 5-25: This section of painted, weathered, and ballasted flextrack proves to be amazingly realistic.

Fig. 5-24: I use Homabed for roadbed.

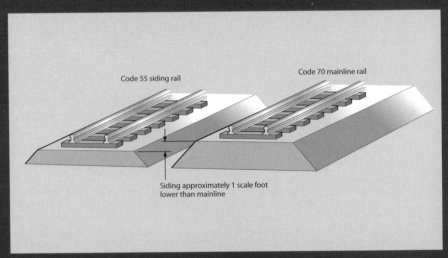

Code 55 siding rail

Code 70 mainline rail

Siding approximately 1 scale foot lower than mainline

Fig. 5-26: Creating a slight difference in elevation from the siding to the main line adds realism to the look of the scene.

Fig. 5-27: Spread Woodland Scenics Subterrain Foam Putty with a 1"-wide putty knife to blend the lower elevation of the siding roadbed into the mainline roadbed.

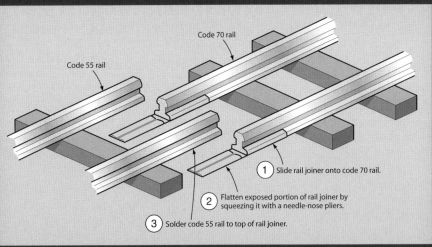

Code 55 rail

Code 70 rail

1 Slide rail joiner onto code 70 rail.

2 Flatten exposed portion of rail joiner by squeezing it with a needle-nose pliers.

3 Solder code 55 rail to top of rail joiner.

Fig. 5-29: To attach code 55 siding rail to code 70 mainline rail, you first slide a rail joiner halfway onto the code 70 rail. Next, flatten the remaining exposed section of rail joiner with a pair of needlenose pliers. Then solder the code 55 rail to the top of the rail joiner.

Fig. 5-28: Once the putty has dried, sand the surface smooth with some fine-grit sandpaper tacked to a homemade sanding block.

Fig. 5-30: Before installing the fishplates to the outside of the rail you should trim off the cast-on spike heads with a hobby knife and an X-acto no. 11 blade.

Fig. 5-31: Apply a dab of five-minute epoxy to the side of the rail and place the fishplate into position.

Fig. 5-32: Paint the ties with inexpensive flat gray primer aerosol paint.

Fig. 5-33: Use a small paintbrush to apply Floquil no. 270-110007 Rail Brown to the sides of the rails.

Fig. 5-34: Brush on a generous wash of India ink and rubbing alcohol (1 part India ink to 1 pint alcohol).

COLORING AND INSTALLING DEEP PROFILE ROCK CASTINGS

Besides an excellent line of model trees, Sterling Models markets a product called Deep Profile rock castings (fig. 5-35). These three-dimensional castings have deep crevasses. They're hollow cast (see fig. 5-36), which cuts down on the weight and makes it easier to cut and fit them to a location if necessary.

The Deep Profile castings are available only as finished castings. All you do is color them prior to installation on a layout.

I used two of the shale castings on the Grand Isle Creamery module. One is shown in fig. 5-37.

Figure 5-38 shows the materials I used to color my rock castings. These consist of four colors of artist's tube acrylics (Raw Sienna, Burnt Umber, Raw Umber, and Mars Black), a stiff-bristled oil painting brush, paper cups, and tap water.

I squeezed about an inch of each acrylic color into a paper cup and then filled the cup with enough tap water to cover the bottom. Starting with the Raw Sienna, Burnt Umber, and Burnt Sienna, I alternately dipped the brush directly into the undissolved acrylic colors and water. I then stippled it onto the dry casting.

I did this alternating each color until they blended together on the rock surface (figs. 5-39 and 5-40). (You may want to practice on a sample before diving into this process since it's a bit of a trial-and-error approach.)

I finished with an application of Mars Black (fig. 5-41). Since it's the most intense of the colors, I diluted it with more water. This made the black run into the crevasses of the rock to highlight them.

Meanwhile, I prepared the location on the module where I intended to install the rock (fig. 5-42). After test-fitting the finished casting (fig. 5-43), I applied some Woodland Scenics Subterrain Foam Putty around it to close any gaps in the scenery base (fig. 5-44).

When the putty had dried, I painted it with the same earth-colored latex paint that I had used to color the rest of the scenery (fig. 5-45). I applied some Weld Bond glue around the perimeter of the casting (fig. 5-46) and pressed it in place on the module (fig. 5-47).

After the Weld Bond had dried, I spackled Ground Goop around the casting (fig. 5-48). I followed that by gluing in place a generous helping of dirt (fig. 5-49).

Fig. 5-35: Even uncolored, this view of the face of one of the Sterling Models shale castings shows its fine deep crevices.

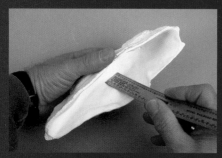

Fig. 5-36: Unlike most rock castings, the Deep Relief castings from Sterling Models are hollow.

Fig. 5-37: Here's a completed Sterling Models rock casting on the Grand Isle module.

Fig. 5-38: To color the castings, you'll need: Raw Sienna, Burnt Umber, Raw Umber, Mars Black artist's tube acrylics, a stiff oil paintbrush, paper cups, and tap water.

Fig. 5-39: Begin the coloring process by dabbing on Raw Sienna with the brush.

Fig. 5-40: After adding splotches of Burnt Umber, do the same with the Raw Umber.

Fig. 5-41: Keep alternating splotches of the previous three colors until you're satisfied with the appearance. Then add a more diluted application of the Mars Black.

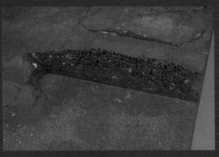

Fig. 5-42: Cut out the area where the casting will be placed. The author paints the scenery base first so no white shows through the ground cover.

Fig. 5-43: Test-fit the rock casting after you've trimmed away the area in the scenery where it will go.

Fig. 5-44: Use Subterrain Foam Putty to fill voids between the scenery base and the casting.

Fig. 5-45: Paint the ground with latex earth-colored paint to prevent any white foam from showing through the ground cover.

Fig. 5-46: Apply Elmer's white glue to the edges of the casting.

Fig. 5-47: Press the casting in place.

Fig. 5-48: I prefer to use Ground Goop as a ground cover base. I use an artist's spatula to apply the material to the surface of the foam.

Fig. 5-49: Apply ground cover—in this case real dirt—and glue it in place.

Power to

Power and telephone lines should be an integral part of any model railroad set in the 20th century. These details aren't difficult or expensive to add to a layout, but many modelers often overlook or fail to finish them properly.

For example, modelers sometimes choose to install plastic poles along their miniature rights-of-way and city streets rather than scale replicas. Or they neglect to use properly sized cross arms.

Too often, modelers don't bother to paint or detail the poles at all. They may not even string wire between them. The net effect of all this is to decrease, rather than increase, realism.

Power company lineman Dick Elwell heads up a pole at Peerless Tanning Company to check out a problem with the service.

the people

When I first visited Dick Elwell's HO scale Hoosac Valley Railroad 25 years ago, I was impressed by his highly detailed poles and lines. Not only were the poles along the right-of-way strung with wires (in this case, thread), but so were the commercial and residential power and telephone poles. This helped bring the layout to life.

When I asked Dick where he had attained his knowledge of pole line construction, he told me he worked as a telephone lineman for New England Telephone Company and had inside information on how to detail pole lines correctly. It was for this reason that I contacted Dick when it came time to prepare the information for this chapter.

BACKGROUND INFORMATION

Before we get started, please keep in mind that it isn't always necessary to replicate every detail I am going to cover to obtain realistic pole lines. Our purpose is to create the illusion of a complete power and phone service system.

There are places on my layout where I didn't bother with many of the finer details. I detailed only those poles in the foreground or around key scenes. This approach cuts down on the work yet makes the layout, as a whole, look better detailed than it is.

Keep in mind that I'm modeling the 1950s. While some aspects of pole and wire layout have remained the same, 21st century pole lines do differ from their mid-20th century counterparts. In many cases today's power and phone service is under

Fig. 6-1: Here we see the detailing of a typical residential power pole. Drop wires are strung from the main power line to the top two receptacles on the transformer. Three (secondary) wires then run from the receptacles on the front face of the transformer to each house receiving service. A number of houses can be connected to one transformer.

Fig. 6-2: Power service to a commercial establishment often requires several transformers to handle the additional service required. These would be mounted on a platform below the cross arms. A three-insulator fixture would be pole-mounted, with wires running from the individual transformers to it. A lateral line would then be run to the structure. It's uncommon to find exterior meters on a larger commercial building. The wires would run down the outside of the structure and enter through the sill plate.

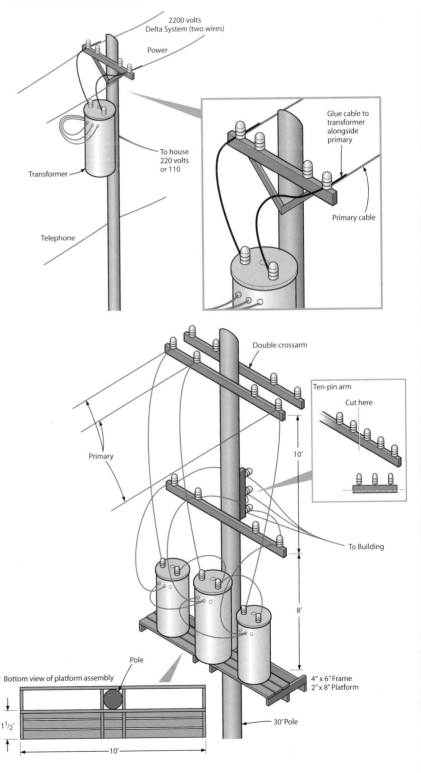

Power Line Transformer Detail

2200 volts
Delta System (two wires)

Power

Glue cable to transformer alongside primary

Transformer

To house 220 volts or 110

Primary cable

Telephone

Double crossarm

Ten-pin arm

Cut here

Primary

10'

To Building

8'

Pole

Bottom view of platform assembly

4" x 6" Frame
2" x 8" Platform

1½'

30' Pole

10'

the ground, negating the use of any poles at all. I wanted to create the look of the power and phone service construction Dick is familiar with. His experience may vary from that of others.

According to Dick, utility poles are generally about 30 feet high. They will almost always carry both power and telephone services. The power lines (consisting of two or three wires) are the uppermost wires on the pole.

To run power to individual dwellings, it first has to be "stepped down" from the primary line's higher voltage to the secondary line's lower voltage. Running it through a transformer takes care of this task.

The transformer is mounted to the pole below the power wires and above the telephone lines. One transformer serves several homes (see fig. 6-1 for wiring details).

The amount of power used by each consumer is registered on a meter box, which is attached to the side of a residence or kept in its basement, preferably where a power company "meter reader" can conveniently read it.

For mills and other large facilities, multiple transformers are pole-mounted, with the primary power run to each of the transformers. Service wires are run from the transformers (fig. 6-2) to the the building where the meters are.

Telephone lines are strung a minimum of eight feet beneath the power lines and fixtures. In urban situations, where the housing is dense, a telephone cable containing many pairs of wires is attached to each pole on a street (fig. 6-3).

The cable enters a terminal box where the pairs are terminated. One terminal box can handle up to 26 customers. Drop wires from the box are run to each dwelling.

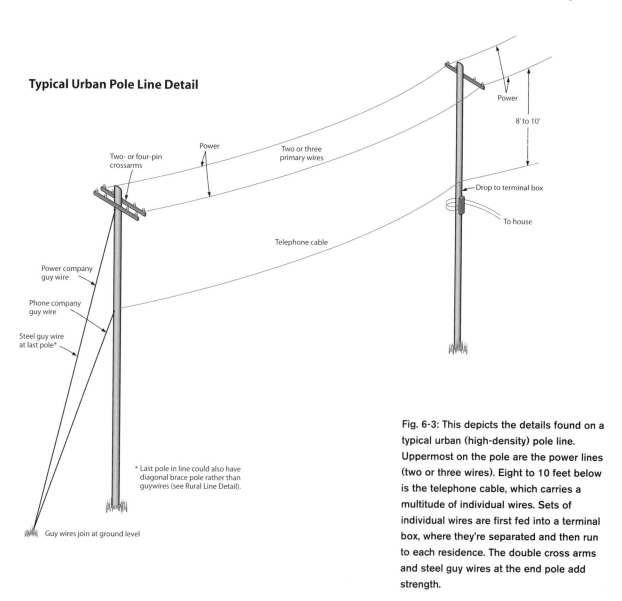

Typical Urban Pole Line Detail

Two- or four-pin crossarms

Power

Two or three primary wires

Power

8' to 10'

Drop to terminal box

To house

Telephone cable

Power company guy wire

Phone company guy wire

Steel guy wire at last pole*

* Last pole in line could also have diagonal brace pole rather than guywires (see Rural Line Detail).

Guy wires join at ground level

Fig. 6-3: This depicts the details found on a typical urban (high-density) pole line. Uppermost on the pole are the power lines (two or three wires). Eight to 10 feet below is the telephone cable, which carries a multitude of individual wires. Sets of individual wires are first fed into a terminal box, where they're separated and then run to each residence. The double cross arms and steel guy wires at the end pole add strength.

In a rural setting, open (or individual) wires are the norm (fig. 6-4). These wires, copper or steel, are strung on a "ten-pin" cross arm (as many as 10 insulators can be mounted on each cross arm).

As with power, telephone service is attached to the dwelling below the eaves of the house, runs down the outside, and enters above the foundation. If the structure is brick or stone, service may enter through a hole drilled in a window frame (see fig. 6-5).

Study figs. 6-3 and 6-4 and you'll see that guy wires or push poles are used on corners, at the end of runs, or where one line intersects another. Power cross arms are doubled on sharp corners or on end poles for additional strength.

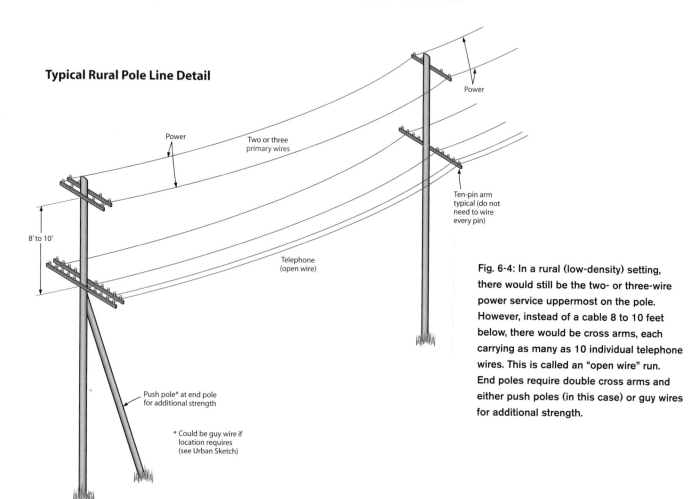

Typical Rural Pole Line Detail

Power

Two or three primary wires

Power

Ten-pin arm typical (do not need to wire every pin)

8' to 10'

Telephone (open wire)

Push pole* at end pole for additional strength

* Could be guy wire if location requires (see Urban Sketch)

Fig. 6-4: In a rural (low-density) setting, there would still be the two- or three-wire power service uppermost on the pole. However, instead of a cable 8 to 10 feet below, there would be cross arms, each carrying as many as 10 individual telephone wires. This is called an "open wire" run. End poles require double cross arms and either push poles (in this case) or guy wires for additional strength.

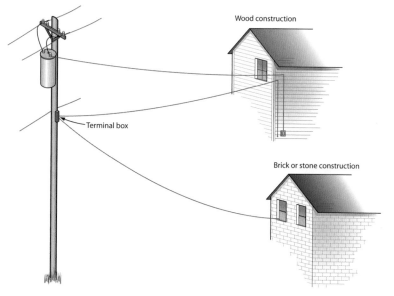

Fig. 6-5: Laterals to residential customers are run from the pole to just below the eaves of each home. The lines are run down the outside of the structure where, in the case of power, there's a meter box. The telephone line may enter the building through the sill plate above the foundation or pass through a 4- by 6-inch lightning protector box mounted outside before entering. On brick buildings, phone service typically enters at a second-floor window through a hole drilled in the outer casing.

Wood construction

Terminal box

Brick or stone construction

ADDING THESE DETAILS

I use Rix Power Plus Products nos. 628-30 40-foot poles (628-30) and 628-35 clear green cross arms for my telephone lines. Rix also sells brown cross arms (no. 628-31), though I prefer the clear green cross arms because of the realistic color of the insulators (it is necessary to hand-paint the assemblies).

I begin pole construction by drawing a razor saw along the length of each pole to distress the surface. Next I glue the cross arms in place.

I brush-paint the pole and cross arms with Polly Scale no. 270-110081 Earth, being careful not to get any paint on the insulators. Then I brush on a wash of India ink and rubbing alcohol (1 teaspoon ink to 1 pint alcohol).

Finally, I dry-brush the lower portion of the pole with Weber-Costello dark gray and black dry pigments to represent the heavy accumulation of creosote in that area. Figure 6-6 depicts the results of each step from left to right.

I use Selley Finishing Touches no. 675-637 line pole transformers for residential service. I glue them to each pole, as required, with two-part epoxy.

For the multiple-transformer assembly, such as that depicted in fig. 6-2, I opted for one Selley no. 675-257 large transformer flanked by two 675-637 models. For Peerless Tanning, I attached the (three-wire) secondary feed from the poles to an SS Limited no. 650-2331 industrial power head fixture on the side of the building.

Lacking a supplier for electrical meters, I made my own from Plastruct nos. 570-90746 strip styrene and 570-90860 rod styrene. I used a NorthWest Short Line cutter to cut the strip stock into 1-foot lengths and the rod stock into 6-inch lengths.

I painted the individual lengths of strip stock with Polly Scale no. 270-414197 D&H Gray to represent the steel body of the meter box. Then I glued the pieces of rod stock to them to represent the glass portion of the assembly (fig. 6-7).

Needing something to represent the telephone terminal boxes, I used 12-inch sections of Central Valley rail fence gates since I have dozens of them lying in the bottom of my scrap box. Figure 6-8 shows the transition from gate to terminal box starting from the left. I painted the boxes with Polly Scale no. 270-110100 Old Silver.

MATERIALS

Plastruct
570-90746 1.0- by 3.2-mm styrene strip
570-90860 1.0-inch by 2.5-mm styrene round rod

Rix Power Plus Products
628-30 40-foot poles
628-35 clear green cross arms

Selley Finishing Touches
675-637 line pole transformers
675-257 large transformers

SS Limited
650-2331 industrial power head

Miscellaneous
All-purpose light green sewing thread
Dual-duty black cotton quilting thread
Heavy-duty black button/carpet thread

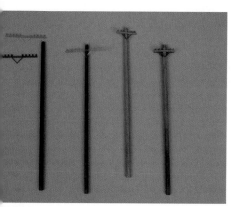

Fig. 6-6: I used Rix 40-foot poles and clear green cross arms for pole assemblies. Left to right: unpainted poles and cross arms, distressed poles with cross arms attached, painted assemblies with the cross arms trimmed, and a finished pole weathered with dry colors.

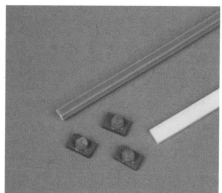

Fig. 6-7: I make my electrical meters from Plastruct 1.0- by 3.2-mm styrene strip (no. 570-90746) and 1.0-inch by 2.5-mm styrene rod (no. 570-90860).

Fig. 6-8: I make my junction boxes from discarded Central Valley fence gates (left to right): stock gates, trimmed gates, and junction boxes.

SAGGING AND THREAD

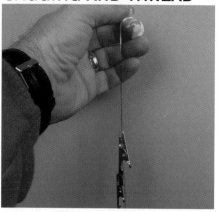

Fig. 6-9: Dip fingers in white glue and drag them along the thread to stiffen it.

I like heavy-duty black carpet/button thread for power and telephone cables and the power laterals from the transformers to the houses. Dual-duty quilting thread works for telephone laterals from the terminal boxes to the houses. We like all-purpose light green sewing thread for replicating open telephone wire.

You also need to create the realistic sag in the thread that's found on real lines. Dick tacks a few 3-to-4-foot lengths of thread to a rafter in his cellar and then attaches a small C-clamp or some alligator clips to the opposite end of the thread.

Then, because real telephone cable is gray, Dick dips a rag in Polly Scale no. 270-110012 Reefer Gray and draws it along the lengths of thread he plans to use for that purpose. (A simpler solution would be to buy gray thread.)

Next, Dick dips his fingers in white glue and draws the glue along all the thread (fig. 6-9). When the glue has dried in a couple of hours, the thread is stiff.

After installing the poles, Dick lays the thread from pole to pole and attaches an alligator clip to each end of the line. He adjusts the

Fig. 6-10: Apply white glue to the power lines at the insulators while the thread is held in place by an alligator clip.

Fig. 6-11: Apply a dab of white glue to the side of the pole where you want to place the telephone cable.

Fig. 6-12: Clip the cable in place with an alligator clip until the glue has dried.

COMPANY CREW AND TRUCK OPTIONS

One detail I wanted to add to my power lines was a line crew doing maintenance work on one of the poles. Thanks to the folks at Woodland Scenics, finding a crew was easy.

The no. 785-1826 City Workers figure set contains two pole line workers. One is equipped with a safety harness and climbs a pole. He snaps right in place on a Rix pole. (Who says things don't go right sometimes?) His partner holds a roll of heavy cable.

The crew needed a vehicle to travel in. One option is the Alloy Forms no. 119-2043 1956 Ford pickup truck with rack and utility boxes. Since I didn't have one lying around, I decided to make my own out of an ER Models no. 262-92133 1950 pickup. Busch makes the same model with working headlights as item no. 189-5643.

I used two sections of Central Valley steel tubular fencing for racks, two lengths

of 1/8-inch-square stripwood for the utility boxes, and sections of .010-inch styrene sheet to represent the access doors on the boxes. A Central Valley ladder topped it off.

Once all the details where glued in

place, I brush-painted everything with Polly Scale no. 270-110040 and weathered it with dry pigments. The illustration shows an out-of-the-box truck with unattached details. The finished truck is on page 58.

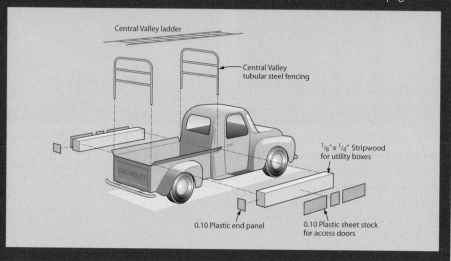

Central Valley ladder

Central Valley tubular steel fencing

1/8" x 1/4" Stripwood for utility boxes

0.10 Plastic end panel

0.10 Plastic sheet stock for access doors

thread until it rests against an insulator on each pole and the proper sag is created.

Once Dick is satisfied with the look of the line, he applies a dab of white glue at each insulator to secure the thread (fig. 6-10). To attach the telephone cable he applies a dab of white glue to one side of each pole (fig. 6-11). He then presses the thread into the glue and clips it to the pole with an alligator clip until the glue has dried (fig. 6-12).

Figure 6-13 shows the detail of the end pole on Fulton Street. Notice the push pole and double cross arms. In fig. 6-14, you can see both the power and telephone lateral lines attached to the houses and the meter box location.

To attach thread to the side of a house, apply white glue to the thread and press it in place. You can also run brass or metal wire, rather than thread, down the side. Be sure it has the same diameter and give it a coat of black paint before gluing it in place.

Figure 6-15 shows the pole that serves Peerless Tanning. Note the double cross arms and the guy wires running from the pole to the ground for extra support.

Fig. 6-13: This end pole on Fulton Street has many details. Note the double cross arms and push pole for added strength, the telephone junction box with lateral wires exiting from it, the drop wires to the transformer, and the lateral power lines running from the transformer to individual houses.

Fig. 6-14: Another view of that pole reveals the lateral power lines attached to the houses just below the eaves, dropping along the outside of the structure, and terminating at the meter boxes. We also can see the telephone laterals attached to the building next to the power line, which drops down the side of the dwelling to just above the foundation.

Fig. 6-15: Here we see the power and telephone service to Peerless Tanning. Since this is an end pole, there is a double cross arm, and double guy wires for more strength. Three transformers handle the additional power necessary for a commercial building such as this one.

Mobile home

While traveling around the country you will most likely see mobile homes. They may be standing alone or in multiple unit parks. They have been part of life in America since the 1920s, particularly since the end of the Second World War.

With this is mind, it makes sense that one or more mobile homes would look appropriate on a layout of the correct period. Fortunately for us, model manufacturers offer a selection of HO replicas to choose from. Let's see how we can put some of them to use.

Canadian National RS-3 no. 3012 passes the Shady Acres trailer park as it heads south along Route 7 on its way to Bennington, Vermont.

heaven

A BIT OF BACKGROUND

Today's single- and double-wide "pre-manufactured" homes are an impressive option for people looking for housing. When it comes to the "double-wide" variety, buyers can opt for one or two stories as well as ranch, Cape Cod, and even colonial styles. Once the units are assembled on their prospective building lots, you'd be hard pressed to distinguish between a pre-manufactured and a site-built dwelling.

It's hard to believe that today's pre-manufactured units had their humble origins in the travel trailers of the 1920s and '30s. Actually, maybe those beginnings weren't so humble after all, as many travel trailers were built with interiors and exteriors resembling what was found on yachts at the time (fig. 7-1). Some trailers even had additions that unfolded from the main body of the unit.

During the Second World War, trailer sales skyrocketed as the units served as housing for thousands of defense workers. Many were built under government contract.

After the war, demand for trailer homes remained high when the returning troops and their families faced shortages in site-built housing. Demand was so high that some firms that had manufactured war material turned to trailer production. One of them was Spartan Aircraft Company, which made the 1947 Spartan Manor model depicted in fig. 7-2.

About this time the industry started pursuing two distinct markets. The first included individuals who longed for the romance of the open road; for them, the travel trailer proved to be the logical alternative. The other market consisted of people looking for a cost-effective way to obtain permanent, on-site housing. They could opt for the single- or double-wide mobile home.

In 1955, the Ventura Company offered a pop-out bay-window model (fig. 7-3) with high ceilings over the living room. They also manufactured wood-sheathed ranch-style homes, although most of their production was of the steel-skinned variety.

According to Allan D. Wallis, the author of *Wheel Estate*, by the end of the last century, mobile homes comprised 25 percent of the housing built annually in the United States. Of those homes, about 46 percent were in mobile home parks.

After the Second World War, most parks were of the "mom and pop" variety that consisted of 40 to 60 spaces. Today, parks average between 150 and 175 spaces.

As mobile homes took on a permanent, on-site character, it didn't take long for owners to start adding site-built additions (fig. 7-4). As Wallis states, "An ensemble of houses and additions looked more like a product of a collision."

Fig. 7-1: In 1922, aviation pioneer Glenn Curtiss designed a custom trailer called the Aerocar. It featured four Pullman car-style berths, a full kitchen, and an observatory with a glass roof similar to airplane cockpits of the period. Courtesy *Wheel Estate* by Allan D. Wallis

Fig. 7-2: After the Second World War, the Spartan Aircraft Company of Tulsa, Oklahoma, turned to house trailers to offset the loss of war materiel production. Here is a 1947 Spartan Manor model. Courtesy *Wheel Estate* by Allan D. Wallis

Fig. 7-3: This 1955 Ventura mobile home features a pullout bay window, a feature often seen on today's travel trailers. Courtesy *Wheel Estate* by Allan D. Wallis

Fig. 7-4: This mobile home in New Castle, Colorado, has a site-built addition that in Allan D. Wallis's words, "Looks like a product of a collision!" Courtesy *Wheel Estate* by Allan D. Wallis

MULTIPLE ELECTRIC METER BOXES

In the previous chapter, I discussed mounting meter boxes on the side of each dwelling. In trailer parks, however, power companies often place meters in a common location for convenience (see figs. 7-23 and 7-24).

I replicated that practice using two Rix poles and a piece of scrap styrene sheet (see fig. 7-25). The meters were scratch-built using techniques described in the previous chapter. The conduit to and from the meters was made from sections of Central Valley no. 270-1601 tubular steel fencing (fig. 7-26).

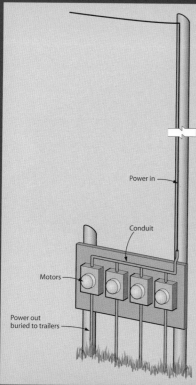

Fig. 7-25: Here are the two Rix poles and the styrene "plywood" attached to each with four meters in place. Wires carrying power to the meters would come down the pole on the right and pass through the conduit to each meter. The power out would travel through wiring enclosed in the conduit, passing into the ground from the meters. The wires would run underground to each trailer.

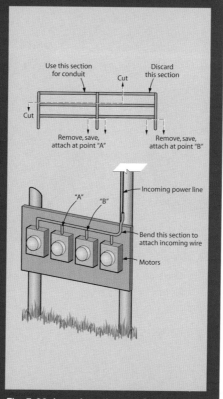

Fig. 7-26: I used sections of Central Valley tubular steel fencing to represent conduit. Remove the sections as indicated and re-attach the short lengths at the bottom to points "A" and "B." Use a pair of pliers to bend the incoming section of conduit.

MATERIALS

City Classics
195-113 Robert's road mobile home

Central Valley
A. 210-1601 fencing

NuComp Miniatures
534-871001 mobile home utility/office trailer
534-871003 mobile home 1
534-871005 mobile home with tip out (enclosed entry)
534-871006 mobile home 2
534-871007 mobile home with porch 2
534-87501 accessory set

Preiser
590-10369 street café people
590-10430 tourists resting
590-10463 hobby gardeners
590-10464 lawn mowers
590-80904 figures

Scenic Express
EXP-881B summer lawn flock and turf
SF-71123 Silflor late summer medium lawn
SF-72023 Silflor late summer high pasture

SS Limited
650-2017 barrels
650-2308 tires
650-2313 brooms
650-2314 trash cans
650-2340 flower pots
650-2403 trash cans
650-2411 fuel oil tanks
650-2449 cans
650-2518 ladders
650-5131 couch
650-5132 chair
650-5153 claw-leg tub

Woodland Scenics
785-49 green blended turf
785-1831 active people
785-1841 cats and dogs

MINIATURE MOBILE HOMES

This information can prove worthwhile to any modeler trying to create a realistic scene from any era between the 1920s and today. House trailers have been seen either being transported on or situated alongside American roadways for decades.

Trailers might be grouped together in a trailer park, standing alone in a field, or rolling down a highway behind an automobile of the period modeled. Also, adding a trailer or mobile home to a farm scene makes sense while increasing its visual interest.

What could be more appealing than a site-built addition? Using one of the mobile-home models

that's now available and adding stick-built additions, a modeler could create an interesting scene without taking up a lot of space.

For my mobile home park I used the five models from NuComp Miniatures that are shown in figs. 7-5, 7-6, 7-7, and 7-8 (nos. 534-871003, -871007, -871006, -871005, and -871001). Although NuComp describes these as mobile homes from the 1970s, my research suggests they could also be used for a layout set in the 1960s.

By incorporating aftermarket details and additions you will increase the visual appeal of these models. For example, I added porch roofs (taken from two City

Classics no. 195-113 Robert's road mobile home) to the trailers in figs. 7-5 and 7-6. I used Central Valley wood fencing to create porch railings for the trailer in fig. 7-5.

Also, I added a couple of scratchbuilt TV antennas to the trailers in figs. 7-5 and 7-8. And I used NuComp's no. 534-871001 mobile home utility/office trailer as an addition to the trailer in fig. 7-6.

Besides the details attached to the trailers themselves, I decided to incorporate many other details to enhance visual interest in the area around the trailers. These are shown in fig. 7-9. Figures 7-10 and 7-11 show how these details bring the scene to life.

Fig. 7-5: NuComp no. 871003 mobile home 1 with a City Classics porch roof and Central Valley fencing railing.

Fig. 7-6: NuComp no. 871007 mobile home with porch 2.

Fig. 7-7: NuComp no. 871006 mobile home 2.

Fig. 7-8: NuComp no. 871005 mobile home with tip out (enclosed entry). I added a City Classics porch roof.

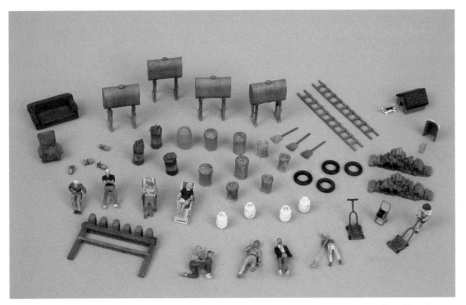

Fig. 7-9: The details the author used for his trailer park include products from City Classics, NuComp, Preiser, SS Limited, and Woodland Scenics. An itemized list is found on page 69 of this chapter.

ADDITIONAL TRAILER OPTIONS

Other trailer options include using City Classics no. 195-113 Robert's road mobile home. Besides the modern mobile homes mentioned here, NuComp Miniatures produces a 1950s-era mobile home park (item no. 534-87150).

Busch has released 1950s-era Airstream trailers in HO scale. They are available individually with a 1950 Buick (item no. 189-44718) or in pairs, along with scenery elements, as a trailer park (item no. 189-19054). BTS offers the no. 464-27405 Junior's Diner that, minus its diner-like accoutrements, can pass as a private residence.

Fig. 7-10: Some of the added details surround these NuComp mobile homes.

Fig. 7-11: Preiser and Woodland Scenics figures help bring this scene to life.

DIGGIN' DITCHES

If you want to add a nice touch to any model scene, just dig a ditch. It's easier to model than you think as long as you use Styrofoam for a scenery base.

On my trailer park module, I decided that a ditch along the main road made sense. So I grabbed my Woodland Scenics foam-cutting knife and carved one (fig. 7-12). I cut short lengths of scrap brass tubing to represent culvert pipes under the driveways to the trailers (fig. 7-13).

Once I had carved the ditch out of the Styrofoam, I applied some ground goop (fig. 7-14). Then I sprinkled dirt over the goop (fig. 7-15).

But that wasn't the end. I dampened the dirt with wet water from a spray bottle (fig. 7-16), added Woodland Scenics no. 785-49 green blended turf (fig. 7-17), and misted on more wet water (fig. 7-18). Using tweezers, I placed the culvert pipe end sections into position (fig. 7-19).

Then I applied a misting of matte medium (1 part matte medium and 5 parts water) to fix everything in place (fig. 7-20). I followed by sprinkling Scenic Express no. EXP-881B summer lawn flocking here and there to represent standing grass (fig. 7-21).

I decided to create the effect of standing water left in the ditches after a rainstorm. Five-minute epoxy works well for this. Just remember to wait until the previous scenery work has completely dried before continuing with this step.

Mix the epoxy as directed, and use a wooden skewer to dab it on the areas you want to look wet (fig. 7-22). I added some old papers from scraps of ads I found in an old magazine. I used Scenic Express Silflor to represent the tall grass found in such areas (see more about this product in chapter 8).

Fig. 7-12: Use a Woodland Scenics foam knife to remove material for the ditch.

Fig. 7-13: Brass tubing serve as culvert pipes under the driveways to each trailer.

Fig. 7-14: Use an artist's spatula to spread Ground Goop over the scenery base.

Fig. 7-15: Sprinkle dirt onto the Ground Goop until it has been thoroughly covered.

Fig. 7-16: Wet the dirt with a misting of "wet water" (water with a couple drops of dishwashing liquid added).

Fig. 7-17: Sprinkle Woodland Scenics no. 785-49 green blended turf on the dampened dirt.

Fig. 7-18: Again, use a spray bottle of wet water to thoroughly wet the surface.

Fig. 7-19: Using tweezers, place the culvert pipes into position.

Fig. 7-20: Apply diluted matte medium (1 part medium to 5 parts water) to the surface of the ground cover with an eyedropper.

Fig. 7-21: Pinch some Scenic Express flocking between your thumb and forefinger. Rub them together while allowing the material to fall onto the surface of the ground.

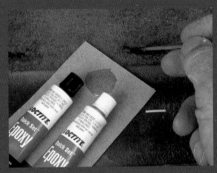

Fig. 7-22: Mix five-minute epoxy as directed and apply it to the bed of the ditch with a wooden skewer to create the look of standing water. It may take two or three coats to achieve the results you desire.

Superdetaile

Anyone who has followed my exploits in the pages of *Model Railroader* or my other books knows I'm a scenery junkie. I'm always looking for new and better ways to increase the realism of my model scenery. I've discovered a few "ready to use" products that make it easier to create excellent scenic effects. Let's take a look at a few of them.

It's early morning at the corner of Spruce and Fulton Streets as a milkman returns to his truck. That's Boston & Maine RS-3 no. 1507 in the distance, preparing to drop a Baltimore & Ohio wagontop boxcar at the Peerless Tanning Company.

d front lawns

THE LOOK OF LAWN

On my Peerless Tanning Company and trailer park modules, I needed a product that would replicate the look of a manicured lawn for the homes along the streets around the mill and trailers (see figs. 8-1 and 8-2). Grass matting never quite left me satisfied.

The folks at Scenic Express have come to the rescue with their no. EXP-881B summer lawn flock and turf (fig. 8-3). It consists primarily of short lengths of static flocking mixed with a small amount of very fine ground foam. It can be purchased in a shaker bottle.

The object of applying flock and turf with a bottle is to create static electric charge as it's shaken. To do this, Scenic Express recommends wrapping the cover of the bottle with self-stick magnetic material.

Although I tried this technique using a piece of magnetic material, I eventually found that when working in confined areas it was easier to apply the flocking by hand. I'd grasp a bit of mixture between my thumb and forefinger and sprinkle it on the previously prepared ground surface.

This method also creates static electricity, which makes many of the flocking strands stand up. As a result, the surface looked like a manicured lawn.

Fig. 8-1: The homeowner on the corner of Fulton and Spruce Streets trims his shrubs as a neighbor takes a stroll with her kids on a summer afternoon in July 1954.

Fig. 8-2: The Butkuses relax on their front porch on this sunny Sunday morning in 1959.

Fig. 8-3: This photo shows Scenic Express no. EXP-881B summer lawn blend of flock and turf.

Fig. 8-4: When working in close quarters use an eyedropper to apply the diluted matte medium to the previously applied ground cover.

Fig. 8-5: Apply the flocking after the glue mixture by rubbing your fingers together while releasing the flocking. Don't apply more glue after this step.

Prepare the surface prior to applying the flocking so that it will stand upright. All the other materials must be in place, and the adhesive that will hold the flocking must be applied ahead of time.

If you try to dribble or spray glue onto the flocking, it will cause the flocking to lie flat. Then you lose the look of upright grass that characterizes a manicured lawn.

In fig. 8-4, I use an eyedropper to apply matte medium around one of my trailers. In fig. 8-5 I squeeze a bit of flocking between my thumb and forefinger while rubbing my fingers together and allowing the flocking to drop onto the previously glued surface.

GREENER PASTURES

While talking to Jim Elster at Scenic Express about various scenery products, he mentioned a material called Silflor. According to Jim, European modelers use it to create different heights, colors, and textures of scale grasses.

Jim sent me a sample pack of Silflor to try (see fig. 8-6). Needless to say, I was pleased with the results. I found that the nos. SF-71123 late summer medium lawn and SF-72023 late summer high pasture suited my modeling needs particularly well.

While you could use the material in large mats, I tore it off in clumps using a pair of tweezers (fig. 8-7). Then I dipped the clumps in full-strength white glue (fig. 8-8) and placed them into position (fig. 8-9). Take a look at figs. 8-10 and 8-11 on the trailer park module for a before-and-after comparison.

Fig. 8-6: I made good use of Silflor from Scenic Express. I like the nos. SF-72023 late summer high pasture and SF-71123 late summer medium lawn.

Fig. 8-7: Use a pair of tweezers to rip off a clump of Silflor.

Fig. 8-8: Dip the Silflor in full-strength white glue.

Fig. 8-9: Place the Silflor into position.

Fig. 8-10: Here we see two trailers before the application of Silflor.

Fig. 8-11: Silflor helped me create the look of tall, unkempt grass in this scene.

FULL-ER BRUSH MAN

In my book *Basic Scenery for Model Railroaders*, I discuss a product called Super Trees that's marketed by Scenic Express. The branch structure of these trees is a material called Filigrane, which gives a realistic representation of the fine branches of smaller trees and brush in HO scale.

However, it takes a bit of work to create a complete "super tree" using the Filigrane as the trunk and colors of Noch leaves as the foliage.

Fortunately, Woodland Scenics has released a product called Fine Leaf Foliage that incorporates the fine branch structure of Filigrane with a pre-applied ground foam leaf material. Now, all you have to do is open the package and plant the trees.

The two Fine Leaf Foliage colors that I found most useful are nos. 785-1131 medium green and 785-1132 light green (fig. 8-12). These work particularly well when used in conjunction with super trees to

represent smaller trees and brush (fig. 8-13).

To install the material, start by breaking off the segment you want (fig. 8-14) and punching a hole in the scenery base with an awl (fig. 8-15). Then dip the Fine Leaf Foliage in a bit of full-strength white glue (fig. 8-16) and place it in position (fig. 8-17).

Fig. 8-12: I like Woodland Scenics nos. 785-1131 medium green and 785-1132 light green fine leaf foliage.

Fig. 8-13: Here we see how the fine leaf foliage adds color and texture to the brush in the foreground at the Grand Isle Creamery.

Fig. 8-14: Use a pair of tweezers to break off a segment of fine leaf foliage.

Fig. 8-15: Punch a hole in the scenery base with a small awl.

Fig. 8-16: Dip the end of the fine leaf foliage into some full-strength white glue.

Fig. 8-17: Place the fine leaf foliage into the previously punched hole.

BIG TREE COUNTRY

I've been scratchbuilding conifer and hardwood trees for my HO scale West Hoosic Division for a number of years now. But for tree-making, like everything else in life, no matter how good you think your techniques may be, there's always someone who knows a better way.

Fortunately, some of these people are willing to share the fruits of their labor, albeit for a price. Two of my favorite suppliers of handmade commercial trees are Jane's Trains in Dallas, Texas, and Sterling Models in Burlington, Vermont. I like these manufacturers because both take a

different approach to tree making, and both excel in their craft. I'll cover some of what they offer on the next two pages.

JANE'S FLASHY FORESTS

Jane's Trains markets both ready-to-plant trees and a product called Forests in a Flash. The latter consist of tree kits, which include enough material (plus instructions) to make six to ten HO scale trees.

Since I'm talking about ready-made trees, I won't delve into the kits other than to say that if you're interested in building your own trees, contact Jane's Trains or go to their website. The firm's mailing and web addresses are listed at the end of the book.

Ready-made trees are available in numerous varieties and sizes. They're really the same trees you would have if you chose to build the kits. Figure 8-18 depicts a smaller (early fall) maple tree, while in fig. 8-19 we see a larger (summer) oak.

In HO scale, the smaller tree stands about 40 feet tall, and the taller one is 45 feet. In fig. 8-20, we see two trees similar to the one in fig. 8-19 on the front lawn of the a house. In fig. 8-21 we see two smaller trees from Jane's Trains framing the driveway of one of our trailers.

Fig. 8-18: A Jane's Trains small (40-foot) maple tree in early fall colors.

Fig. 8-19: A Jane's Trains large (50-foot) oak tree.

Fig. 8-20: Two of Jane's Trains oak trees shade the front lawn of the Peerless Tanning Company owner's house on the corner of Spruce and Fulton Streets in Burlington.

Fig. 8-21: A couple of Jane's Trains 40-foot maple trees flank the entrance to one of the NuComp trailers.

STERLING MODELS

The folks at Sterling Models sell only pre-made trees, but what beautiful specimens they are. There are six varieties of conifers and two of hardwoods. Sterling also makes hardwoods in different foliage colors, ranging from mid-summer to late fall.

Their conifers are some of the most exquisite I have ever seen, particularly the white pines and blue spruces. In fig. 8-22 we see a 46-foot tall blue spruce, while in fig. 8-23 we have a 55-foot-tall white pine.

In the foreground in fig. 8-24, there's a grove of white pines; in the background are a number of aspens. Figure 8-25 shows three types of Sterling Models' trees. On the left are two spruces, above the rock outcropping are three Aspens, and on the right is an early fall maple just starting to change color.

I've heard modelers say that they don't like paying premium prices for trees. Yet they often don't hesitate to pay $200 or $300 for a craftsman kit or $30 to $40 for a freight car that they place on a layout with a ground foam forest that looks like it's filled with green puffballs.

If creating a forest out of high-priced commercial trees turns you

Fig 8-22: A Sterling Models 46-foot blue spruce tree.

Fig 8-23: A Sterling Models 55-foot pine tree.

off, you can take what I call the "highlight" approach (fig. 8-25). This is, rather than fill your woodlands with high-priced trees, use homemade varieties for the majority of the woods while relying on the more expensive specimens to highlight primary structures or scenes.

For example, I use six Sterling Models trees to accent the rock outcropping while the rest of the woods are the homemade variety. (For information on Sterling Models rock outcroppings, refer to chapter 5.)

Fig 8-24: Here we see a grove of large pine trees in the left foreground, with a stand of aspens in the distance to the right.

Fig 8-25: It's early fall, and frost has already caused the leaves on the large maple on the right to turn color. The cold weather has not, however, taken its toll on the aspens above the rock outcropping. The spruce trees to the left will hold their needles through the winter. All of these HO scale trees are commercial products from Sterling Models.

Gallery

REFERENCES

Hambourg, Serge 1988. *Mills and Factories of New England.* Harry N. Abrams Inc., 100 Fifth Ave., New York, New York.

Hudson, John W., II. *Creameries of Upstate New York at the Turn of the Century.* Robert A. Liljestrand, ed. Bob's Photo, 37 Spring Street, Ansonia, CT.

Liljestrand, Robert A. and John Nehrich. *Railway Milk Cars: Volumes 1 & 2.* Bob's Photo, 37 Spring Street, Ansonia, Ct., 06401

McMartin, Barbara with W. Alec Reid 1999.*The Glove Cities: How a People and their Craft Built Two Cities.* Lake View Press, 339 Kasson Drive, Canada Lake, Caroga Lake, New York, 12032

Mohowski, Robert E. 1995. *New York, Ontario & Western Railway and the Dairy Industry in Central New York State: Milk Cars, Mixed Trains, and Motor Cars.* Garrigues House Publishing Company, P.O. Box 400, Laurys Station, Pa., 18059

Nimke, R. W. *The Rutland–60 years of Trying.* Sharp Offset Printing Inc., 10 Cleveland Ave., Rutland, Vermont, 057011

Noble, Allen George 1996. *The Old Barn Book: A Field Guide to North American Barns and Other Farm Structures.* Rutgers University Press, 100 Joyce Kilmer Ave., Piscataway, New Jersey, 08854-8099

R.P.I. New England Berkshire & Western. Website: http://railroad.union.rpi.edu

Wallis, Allan D. 1991. *Wheel Estate (The Rise and Decline of Mobile Homes).* Oxford University Press Inc., 200 Madison Avenue, New York, New York, 10016

SUPPLIERS & MANUFACTURERS

Activa Products Inc. (Celluclay)
512 South Garrett
Marshall, TX 75670
Phone: (903) 938-2224
(800) 883-3899
Fax:(903) 938-3899
www.activaproducts.com

Blaire Line
PO Box 1136
Carthage, MO 64836
Phone: (417) 359-8300

City Classics
P.O. Box 16502
Pittsburgh, PA 15242
Phone: (412) 276-1312
Fax: (412) 276-1312
ctyclsscs@aol.com

Classic Metal Works
3401 Silica Road
Sylvania, OH 43560
Phone: (419) 842-8114
Fax: (419) 842-9845
CMWsales@classicmetalworks.com

C. S. Designs Incorporated (Scale Crete)
140 Brockton Place
Val Paraiso, IN 46385
Phone: (800) 326-7087
LMgaller@comcast.net

Evergreen Hill Models
31328 North Brooks Creek Rd.
Arlington, WA 98223

GHQ (farm equipment)
28100 Woodside Road
Shorewood, MN. 55331
Phone: (612) 374-2693
www.ghqmodels.com

Gold Medal Models
1412 Fisherman Bay Road
Lopez, WA 98261
Fax: (360) 468-2171
www.goldmm.com
goldmedl@rockisland.com

Grandt Line Products
1040B Shary Court
Concord, CA 94518
Phone: (925) 671-0143
Fax: (925) 671-0608
www.grandtline.com
grandt@pacbell.net

Janes Trains
8221 Ferguson Road
Dallas, TX 75228
Phone: (214) 319-7668
(866) 433-TREE (8733)
forestinaflash@hotmail.com
www.forestinaflash.com

Micro Engineering
1120 Eagle Road
Fenton, MO 63026
Orders: (800) 462-6975
Phone: (636) 349-1112
Fax: (636) 349-1180

NuComp Miniatures
P.O. Box 539
Bluffton, IN 46714
Phone: (800) 710-9034
http://nucompinc.com

O&W Shops (Rich Cobb)
109 Cayuga Street
Clyde, NY 14433
Phone: (315) 923-9289
E mail: richinny@hotmail.com
Rcobb@rochesterrr.com

Precision Laser Craft
32 Beekman Drive
Agawam, MA 01001
Phone: (413) 572-0510
Fax: (413) 562-3265
prelasr@aol.com
www.Precisionlasercraft.com

Rix Products
3747 Hogue Road
Evansville, IN 47712
Phone: (812) 426-1749
www.rixproducts.com
Rick@rixproducts.com

Scale Structures Limited (Division of Jaks Industries)
P.O. Box 654
Broomfield, CO 804038
Phone: (303) 279-2253
(800) 352-1552
Fax: (303) 279-9668
www.jaksind.com

Scenic Express
1001 Lowery Avenue
Jeanwette, PA 15644
Phone: (412) 527-7479
(800) 234-9995
www.scenicexpress.com
scenery@attglobal.net

Selley Finishing Touches (Bowser Manufacturing Co.)
1302 Jordan Ave.
P.O. Box 322,
Montoursville, PA 17754
Phone: (570) 368-2379
E mail: wcbecker@aol.com

Sterling Models
P.O. Box 143
Johnson, VT 05656
Scenery@sterlingmodels.com
www.sterlingmodels.com

Wm. K. Walthers
PO Box 3039
Milwaukee, WI 53201
Phone: (414) 527-0770
Fax: (414) 527-4423
www.walthers.com

Woodland Scenics
PO Box 98
Linn Creek, Mo., 65052
Phone: (573) 346-5555
Fax: (573) 346-3768
www.woodlandscenics.com